Organic Tales
— F R O M —
Indian Kitchens

Organic Tales
— F R O M —
Indian Kitchens

WARM SPICE AND EVERYTHING NICE—
HEART-WARMING STORIES AND RECIPES FROM
KITCHEN TABLES IN TWO CONTINENTS

PRIYA MARY SEBASTIAN

I dedicate this book to my parents and siblings
who made growing up so much fun!

I dedicate this book to my parents and siblings who made growing up so much fun!

Table of Contents

A Note from the Author
March 16, 2020

A s I write this, the coronavirus is rampaging through America and the rest of the world. Because of its highly contagious nature, we are in a state of lockdown. I turned off India Café's "OPEN" sign at the end of dinner service on March 14, not knowing when I would be able to resume operations again. Cities and states have closed businesses, hotels, and places of worship. Public gatherings of more than fifteen people are not recommended and, in many cases, forbidden. Fear is everywhere. Older people are particularly vulnerable, but the disease has also ravaged young people and even children.

People are forced to keep their distance from one another and most of us have become fastidious about hand hygiene. Sanitizers, toilet paper, and paper towels are flying off grocery shelves, and in many cases those shelves are empty. Grocery stores can barely keep items like frozen foods and chicken in stock.

Most of us are self-quarantining. Away from our normal routines of visiting friends, going out to eat, parties, and religious observances, a certain listlessness has set in. It is at this time that we have started to rethink a concept as old as time—the family dinner table. In our hectic lives, we have often forgotten about it and its comforting familiarity. Suddenly, this aspect of our lives had a greater significance in what it stood for—nourishing meals prepared together and enjoyed together sprinkled with stories and a great deal of laughter!

After all, food is an outward expression of the greater culture of any people.

Just as my grandmother used to tell me stories of the days of the maharajas and their wives (some of whom she had met as part of my grandfather's official capacity). To me, a modern girl who, unlike her, played tennis and badminton with boys and swam in pools wearing scandalous (in her eyes) swimsuits, the stories might as well have been fairytales for all the resemblance they had to my regular life! In the same way, the stories I tell of a childhood in immediate post-independence India, probably seem to my kids and grandkids like they come from another century. But tell them I must for, in doing so, I am giving them a better understanding of myself.

This virus too will pass. People will recover and move on with their lives. The stock market will bounce back again, and life will return to normal. I will see India Café's "OPEN" sign lit up brighter than before. In the meantime, just like the old-time Londoners huddled in their homes waiting for the bubonic plague to pass, I too will spend this time in reflection in the sanctuary of my home. All the chaos surrounding us has only managed to highlight the most important aspects of human life—the warmth of a loving family and the comfort of the family dining table. Even in the midst of despair, the family table is a constant presence, and provides us with hope and sustenance just as it has throughout the ages!

~ Priya Mary Sebastian

Prologue

My *mom always wanted me to write a book,* but when I expressed doubts about whether people might feel offended by references in the book, she would always say, "Aaaay, they won't mind. You just go ahead." She was my staunchest ally and the person who believed the most in my ability to write a book. I always tried to but never got around to it. She passed away two years ago. I can only hope that the book I have written will make her proud. I can almost see her in my mind sitting with the book with a gleeful expression on her face that what she said turned out to be true. As I get older, I spend a lot of time reliving every aspect of our life together, when we were a family of seven—five kids, dad and mom. In our house, dinner time was a special occasion as we collected around the oval dining table with its glass surface. Dad would ask each of us what we had done that day, and all of us would collectively make our comments about the food that mom had so carefully prepared. There would be rice, a curry with gravy, meat or fish, and the vegetable of the day. And we were all foodies! We had plenty to say about the food we ate. If something was not up to snuff, dad would start with, "What rubbish is this?" And each one would have their own take on it. So while the chef in a restaurant has to face only one Michelin critic, my poor mother had to endure six Michelin critics at the same time! But she took it all in stride and always tried to balance our nutrition and taste. Before going to school, the last thing she would do would be to plant a kiss on our cheek and put two calcium Sandoz tablets in our mouths so that we would become taller than her little five-foot self! So, my dearest mother, I dedicate this book to your memory and to the good care you took of all of us. Thank you from the bottom of my heart, always with love.

Your daughter,
Priya

1
Malu's Fish Curry

I *can still see her sweet, smiling, round face.* Clad in her knee-length plaid Dhoti, her blouse showing off most of her midriff, with the nose ring glinting on her nose, Malu came to work for my mother-in-law every morning from her little hut at the border of our property. It is a hut she shared with three grown-up children and their families. She would come bursting with village news over the sandy soil, striding past the coconut trees swaying in the breeze. The first thing she would do was to get out the old rice and make a porridge out of it, which she would eat with the leftover curry. That was her breakfast. She would squat on the ground and eat it with her hand. Having finished, she would let out a big belch and was then ready for the day's work. There was breakfast to be made, usually puri, puttu, uppuma, dosa, or some other rice flour delicacies. Through it all, there would be a running commentary of who fell off the coconut tree, the village girl who got pregnant, or other juicy gossip from the village.

Breakfast done, Malu would put on her attire suitable for going to the market. This consisted of a white sari that covered her bosom and gave her dignity. Another adornment was her chappals, sandals so worn out that their straps made wide arcs on her feet. Thus attired, she would hurry to the market to get the best catch of the day and bring it home to cook. When she came home with the fish she had purchased, my mother-in-law would ask, "Ethra aayi?" ("How much was it?") Then Malu would inform her that although the fishermen had asked for a high price, she had bargained him down. Of course, being the frugal housewife, my mother-in-law would chide her, saying, "Nee chodichathu koduthittu vanno?" ("You just gave him what he asked and came home?") This was almost a daily interaction.

Then it was time to clean the fish. She would carefully take off her outer sari and hang it in the little room by the side of the back veranda where dry coconuts were kept. And then on an age-old piece of wood that had seen many a groove from previous choppings, Malu would first scale the fish, gut it, and finally make it into small steaks. Then she would proceed to make the curry in the wide mud pot that had been seasoned with many another fish curry. I can still smell the aroma of the curry with its fresh curry leaves.

Malu's Fish Recipe

Ingredients:

2 pounds of fish (either steaks or fillet of fish made into steak-size pieces)

3 tablespoons vegetable oil

3 tablespoons coconut oil

2 teaspoons dark mustard seeds

6 dry chili pods

2 tablespoons curry leaves

1 chopped onion

3 tablespoons chopped cilantro

6 chopped garlic cloves

2 chopped green chilies

Finger-length chopped ginger

1 teaspoon turmeric powder

2 teaspoons chili powder

1 tablespoon coriander powder

1 teaspoon garlic powder

1 teaspoon ground black pepper

1 teaspoon onion powder

½ teaspoon methi (fenugreek) powder

1 tablespoon apple cider vinegar

1 can crushed tomato

2 cans of coconut milk

2 cans water

salt to taste

In a wide saucepan, take 3 tablespoons of vegetable oil and 3 tablespoons of coconut oil and when the oil is hot, add 2 teaspoons of mustard seeds, six dry chili pods, and a handful of curry leaves. When you hear the mustard popping, add 1 chopped onion, 3 *tablespoons of chopped cilantro, six chopped garlic cloves, two chopped green chilies, and a finger length of ginger peeled and chopped into the oil. Sauté this until the onions turn translucent and then add salt to taste, 1 teaspoon turmeric powder, 2 teaspoons chili powder, 1 tablespoon coriander powder, 1 teaspoon of garlic powder, 1 teaspoon of ground black pepper, 1 teaspoon of onion powder, and half a teaspoon of methi (fenugreek) powder. Sauté all this until deep brown and then add 1 tablespoon of apple cider vinegar, one can of crushed tomato, two cans of coconut milk and two cans of water. This will create a yellow gravy, and into this add 2 pounds of your favorite fish steaks. Stir a couple of times, cover the pan, then heat on medium and cook it for five minutes. Your fish is done. Serve it over hot white rice.*

P.S: You can use any kind of fish including salmon, mackerel, swordfish, tilapia, catfish, or red snapper.

2
Grandma Thresia's Chicken Curry

A*s you enter the brick brown gate* of the house on Sullivan Street, far from the hustle and bustle of the main road, the first thing that strikes you about the house is the long stairways leading up to the entrance and the imposing columns in front. It was built in the Portuguese style of architecture at a time when Madras (I still like to call it Madras and not Chennai) was heavily influenced by either the British or the Portuguese. The spacious veranda has its swinging salon doors at the two ends, one leading into the small dining room with an adjoining kitchen. From the small kitchen, there were the myriad steps leading down to the separate annex away from the main house, six rooms in all. Most of these rooms were used by the young bachelors in the house, but the most spacious one of all was the kitchen with the wood-burning stoves.

This was my grandmother's domain. Grandma Thresia was a formidable person, a brilliant cook, a great socialite, and one of the best dressed ladies of the time. She knew everyone who was anybody in Madras, she knew all the latest styles in clothes and jewelry, and to her servants she was absolute terror! With a withering look, she could send her scullery maids scrambling for cover. She did not suffer fools gladly. Meals at Grandma Thresia's were special occasions and she always fed us like we were going to be sent out to famine-ravished lands afterwards. You could smell her cooking on the veranda wafting in from the open window of the kitchen. Since she cooked on a kerosene stove upstairs, you could smell the fuel mixed with the scent of curry. When lunch was served in the small dining room with its English side boards with all the English China arranged on it, everyone gathered around the table. My grandfather, who was a lawyer, had his office off to the side of his bedroom with an attached annex for his stenographer. This room had so many cabinets filled with dusty files. My earliest memories were of the typewriter clacking away and my grandfather pouring over his law books. He would join us too, and he was notorious for his sense of humor. Sometimes his kind, low-key sense of humor, especially when it was directed at her food, did not sit so well with my grandmother.

This chicken curry, like many chicken curries in India in my day, was guest food. When a chicken was run down, caught, dispatched with quick ease, and later dipped in hot water and stripped of its feathers, we knew a guest was coming to dinner. It was a special occasion. The chicken would be quartered and made into small pieces, having been gutted and beheaded. No edible part was ever wasted including the neck, the ovary sack, the stomach, or its unformed eggs. These were delicacies kids in India fought over. No one was crazy about the breast meat, because most people preferred the thighs and legs.

Grandma Thresia's Chicken Curry

Ingredients:

2 pounds of chicken thighs, bone in, skinless with every piece cut into two

1 large onion, chopped

2 tablespoons cilantro, chopped

2 tablespoons curry leaves

2 green chilies, chopped

6 cloves of garlic, chopped

half a finger length of ginger, peeled and chopped

salt to taste

2 teaspoons turmeric powder

4 teaspoons chili powder

6 teaspoons coriander powder

1 can of coconut milk

1 tablespoon of apple cider vinegar

4 cans of water

4 large potatoes, peeled and quartered

1 teaspoon ground black pepper

1 teaspoon garlic powder

1 teaspoon onion powder

Pour the oil into a large saucepan on medium heat and add the onions, cilantro, curry leaves, green chilies, garlic, and ginger and sauté until translucent. Then add the salt, turmeric powder, chili powder, coriander powder, ground black pepper, onion powder, and garlic powder. Do not let it burn. When it is medium brown in color, add the vinegar and coconut milk. Stir gently and add

7

the rest of the water too. To this mixture, add your chicken and potatoes and mix it thoroughly. Cover the pan and cook it for 25 minutes, stirring occasionally so that the potatoes don't stick to the bottom. You will have a nice thick chicken curry that can be served over rice or eaten with naan.

3

Mummy's Batter-Fried Prawns

My father worked for J&P Coats, a multinational corporation. As part of the perks, every summer we had use of the company guesthouse, Iron House, in a hill town called Kodaikanal. It was a hill station so far above sea-level that the weather was cool during the day time and almost became chilly at night. This was a welcome relief from the hot summers of the Indian plains. The house came with its own servants' quarters, cook, and gardener. Iron House was unique because it was basically a church that was turned into a summer house. It had two wings with the lofty arches of the church and creaky wooden floors. Of course, it came with its own ghostly tales too. We kids used to have unending fun while going to sleep reminding each other of the ghosts that lurked nearby that made the floorboards creak at night!

Kodaikanal was a relaxing vacation spot. One could go hiking, boating, and horse riding. And for avid golfers like my father and brothers, Kodaikanal also boasted of a great golf course where the bison came in the night and left their footprints. It was great fun. Part of the fun were the great meals that mom always cooked up. When my mom was in the kitchen, the cook who came with the house was reduced to being the onion chopper. She would meticulously plan out all the meals, and we had a family that really enjoyed food. She and dad would go to the local market and get the best fish, usually a carp variety from the nearby lake called Varaal, and make great curries with it. As an appetizer, she sometimes batter fried shrimp for all of us. You can imagine the commotion as each of us tried to get the maximum share! Her grandchildren especially enjoyed these vacations.

At our last family vacation together in Kodaikanal, my mother as usual had woken up early to supervise our breakfast. My daughter, then a young teenager, was also an early riser. So Ammamma, as my mother was called by her grandkids, took my daughter Kavya to the larder and pointed triumphantly to the ground near the door of the larder saying, "Kavya, the garlic has moved!" They were playing their own Sherlock Holmes games. My mother had been suspecting that the cook was helping himself to the provisions in the larder for some time. He would somehow manage to palm it off to his lazy, corpulent wife who lived in their small house away from the main house. So my mother had taken it upon herself to prove her theory. She had placed a bulb of garlic behind the closed door of the larder and the next morning, to her absolute glee, discovered that the garlic had moved several inches. Gotcha! She needed to share it with someone, and her granddaughter, whose imagination was as vivid as her own, was the ideal person.

10

Mummy's Batter-Fried Prawns

Ingredients:

2 pounds large shrimp, peeled and deveined

½ cup all-purpose flour

1 teaspoon baking powder

salt to taste

1 teaspoon garlic powder

1 teaspoon ground black pepper

1 teaspoon onion powder

2 tablespoons soy sauce

2 tablespoons hot sauce

1 egg

1 tablespoon sour cream

3 cups of vegetable oil to fry

Mix the shrimp with all the ingredients. In a wok, pour 3 cups of oil and bring it to 350°F. Drop the coated shrimp one at a time, making sure not to drop too many at once so that the oil in the pan does not lose its temperature. When the shrimp turn golden brown, it is time to take them out and blot them in a plate lined with a paper towel. They are best enjoyed while hot along with any number of chutneys and sauces—cilantro chutney, date chutney, Yum Yum sauce, and even plain old ketchup.

4

Amma's Mutton Korma

As you turn on the dirt road from Pavaratti town to the rice paddy fields, you can see the white wall of my in-laws' home. The walls are overrun with a bower of Bougainvilleas, and a profusion of pink and white flowers cascade down. Then there is the inevitable bunches of chethipoo (Ixora Coccinea), a vision in red. Beyond that comes the house that is set among the serenity of coconut trees. The soil is sandy and feels like the beach under your feet. It is a beautiful home, and the back porch is enclosed with an airy lattice of grills. It also boasts a hanging swing that can comfortably accommodate two sitting adults or one adult lying down. It was great for having a talk.

My mother-in-law's kitchen had two sides—one for the wood-burning stoves and the other for the gas stove. The wood-burning part was used to cook rice in great big pots over firewood chopped from the yard. Every part of the coconut tree was fair game for firewood, and it was Malu the maid's job to gather it in her free time. My mother-in-law, or Amma as she was affectionately called, was a great cook. Her repertoire was not overwhelming, but what she cooked was close to perfection. One such dish was her mutton curry. Now, mutton was an expensive commodity, probably the most expensive of all the meats. Being a poor country, the people needed proof that it was indeed mutton that they were paying for and not some other animal. So the butcher would ceremoniously hang the carcass on a hook in his shop and have the head of the animal lying on the counter very nonchalantly as proof. So, as you can imagine, mutton was usually purchased when guests came to dine. It was a treat that became more frequent in my mother-in-law's house after my husband's sister got married. The new son-in-law did not eat beef and liked only mutton. Of course, that was reason enough for everyone in the house to scramble and make sure mutton was served for most meals. It would be a thick, rich gravy usually served with rice, but it can also be served with chappathees or naan.

Amma's Mutton Korma

*In India mutton usually refers to goat meat but lamb can be substituted just as well.

Ingredients:

2 pounds of mutton with a little bit of fat

2 large onions, chopped

2 tablespoons curry leaves

6 cloves of garlic, chopped

1 finger length of ginger, chopped

salt to taste

2 teaspoons turmeric

4 teaspoons chili powder

6 teaspoons coriander powder

6 cardamom pods

2 star anise

1 teaspoon cumin seeds

6 cloves

2 sticks of cinnamon

1 cup grated unsweetened coconut

1 can of coconut milk

½ cup coconut oil

1 teaspoon garlic powder

1 teaspoon ground black pepper

1 teaspoon onion powder

1 tablespoon apple cider vinegar

¼ cup of water

Wash the mutton especially well, rubbing it with a little salt and washing it out with water, which will take away any of the gamey smell. In a pressure cooker, place the mutton along with salt, 1 teaspoon of turmeric, 1 teaspoon of chili powder, 1 teaspoon of garlic powder, 1 teaspoon of ground black pepper, one teaspoon of onion powder and a tablespoon of apple cider vinegar. Mix it well and add one fourth cup of water and place it on the burner at medium-high. When the pressure starts to go from the top, put the weight of the cooker on and turn it to medium and cook it for about 12 minutes if it is lamb or 20 minutes if it is goat meat. This will ensure that the meat is tender.

In a coffee grinder, grind the cardamom, cumin, cloves, cinnamon, and star anise until it is a fine powder. Add half of the coconut oil to the saucepan and bring it to medium heat. Sauté the garlic, ginger, grated coconut, and half the onions until the mixture turns brown. It has to be stirred constantly or it is likely to burn. To the browned mixture, add 1 teaspoon of turmeric, 3 teaspoons of chili powder, 6 teaspoons of coriander powder, and the mix of ground cardamom, cumin, cloves, cinnamon, and star anise. After giving it a few stirs, turn off the stove and pour the mixture into a blender. Blend until smooth (make sure to cover the blender with a cloth or the hot mixture will fly everywhere and may even cause burns!). In the same saucepan, heat the rest of the coconut oil and sauté curry leaves and the other half of the onions. When browned, throw in the meat and the blender mixture of spices, pour in the can of coconut milk, and on medium heat bring it to a light boil. Your korma is ready.

5

Lissy's Beef Cutlets

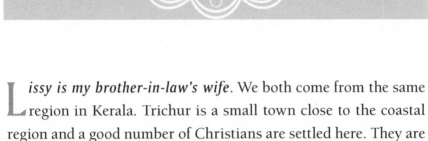

L issy is my brother-in-law's wife. We both come from the same region in Kerala. Trichur is a small town close to the coastal region and a good number of Christians are settled here. They are a unique lot who call themselves Syrian Catholics, and while some of them trace their ancestry to the Nostroni Christians of Syria, others believe that their ancestors were converted by the apostle Thomas when he came to the coastal town in Kerala. Regardless, they have customs that are unique, like mass being celebrated in the Syrian language and many of their dishes having Middle Eastern origins. It is a Catholic culture that you will find nowhere else, and the town boasts a cathedral that is supposed to be a scaled-down version of the famous Notre Dame in Paris.

Lissy, my sister-in-law (in India they call the brother-in-law's wife a "co-sister") has a background similar to my own. Culturally, we have a lot in common, and we even went to the same colleges a few years apart. College is a very ambitious term to use for these institutions because although the curriculum could stand up to any international university, the personal development standards were only that of a high school. Of course, we went to college at the age of fifteen so maybe it was just appropriate that they treated us like school kids! The nun in charge of us was called the hostel warden, and her only job was to make sure we did not get into trouble, that we studied at the appropriate times, and went to church when we were supposed to. This also meant that we behaved like immature schoolgirls and were curious enough to sneak into the warden's room to see if nuns wore bras. "Trouble," according to the hostel warden, was nothing very earth shattering. It can be as simple as looking out of the corridor window that was heavily draped because it meant that you were looking at the boys seated in neat rows on the walls of the engineering college across the road. That was the height of impropriety in those days! So Lissy and I knew a lot of mutual friends who were also alumni of this noble institution whose claim was to cultivate scholars who were also model housewives.

Both of us were married in the arranged marriage system (which meant that the family chooses the bride and groom) to brothers who are both physicians in the United States. Every Christmas we felt the need to travel several hundred miles across the United States so that our families could meet and celebrate Christmas with our own unique traditions and, of course, food. We continued this for thirty-five years until the kids grew up and had families of their own, which made it impossible to continue this tradition. But whenever we gathered, Lissy and I had so much to talk about—mutual friends, relatives, and the old institution.

In fact, we laughed so much that the children had a name for us: "The Laughing Buddies." So I thought I would share my good friend and co-sister's very tasty cutlet recipe.

Lissy's Beef Cutlets

Ingredients:

2 pounds of ground beef (preferably with a 70/30 ratio of fat)

salt to taste

2 teaspoons garlic powder

2 teaspoons ground black pepper

1 teaspoon onion powder

2 tablespoons apple cider vinegar

3 large potatoes, peeled and cubed

2 tablespoons coconut oil

1 large onion, chopped

8 garlic cloves, chopped

4 green chilies, chopped

finger length of ginger, peeled and chopped

3 tablespoons curry leaves

2 teaspoons turmeric powder

2 teaspoons chili powder

1 teaspoon of garam masala

6 cardamom pods

2 sticks of cinnamon

6 cloves

3 pieces of star anise

2 containers of breadcrumbs (panko will be more crunchy)

8 eggs

3 cups of vegetable oil for frying

In a saucepan, break up the ground beef and add salt, ground black pepper, garlic powder, onion powder, and the apple cider vinegar. Brown the beef, stirring occasionally, and when it is cooked through, run it through a colander to drain out any excess fat. Place the beef in a food processor and give it a few spins until it is smooth and even. Do not over-grind or you will lose the texture. In another pot, cook your potatoes in water and salt for about 15 minutes until tender and then drain them. Mash the potatoes. In a coffee grinder, thoroughly grind the cardamom, cloves, cinnamon, and star anise. Then sauté the onions, garlic, green chilies, ginger, and curry leaves in the coconut oil until translucent. Add the turmeric, chili powder, garam masala, and the spices that were powdered in the coffee grinder. Add the beef and the potatoes to this mixture and keep aside for it to cool. When sufficiently cool, mix it thoroughly and form it into oval-shaped patties half an inch thick. In a bowl, beat the eggs well and use another bowl to hold your breadcrumbs. Dip the patty first into the eggs and then into the breadcrumbs. With your hands, make sure the breadcrumbs adhere to the patty well. In a deeper saucepan, pour the 3 cups of vegetable oil and bring it to a temperature of 350°. Place the cutlets gently and fry them on both sides until golden brown. When done, place them on a tray lined with paper towels. This can be either a snack or dinner and can be served with red onions marinated in apple cider vinegar or any other relish.

6

Vinoo's Hutterite Duck Roasted with Spring Potato

My youngest brother Vinoo is a nephrologist in Great Falls, Montana. He and his family are all foodies, always going the extra mile to try something exotic and new. It must have come from the time when he was stationed in Guam, which is a tropical paradise. They became experts on sushi with all the abundance of fresh seafood available there. Even his little daughter, at that time barely five years old, declared that sushi was her favorite food! Apart from his duties as a physician, my brother is an avid hunter and fisherman. He makes the most tender steaks from venison or bison. Great Falls is blessed with a lot of natural beauty and the Blackfoot riverbed behind his cabin in Lincoln is paved with stones of such natural beauty and color that I have brought them back for my aquarium. Part of his work as a physician involves going to the Indian settlement in Browning. The Hutterites are a community who live around this area and farm the land. They are a traditional people farming in the ways of their forefathers, and while all of us are trying very hard to buy produce that is deemed organic, the Hutterites probably do not know any other way of farming. My brother, ever the foodie, figured out that this community raises the best ducks. Plump and juicy, they are a far cry from the scrawny, over-frozen ducks available on the supermarket shelves. Whenever we visit my brother, he makes sure that we come back home with at least two frozen ducks in our luggage.

Vinoo's Hutterite Ducks Roasted with Spring Potato

Ingredients:

1 duck

2 pounds of spring potatoes

salt to taste

4 teaspoon garlic powder

4 teaspoons black pepper

2 teaspoon onion powder

2 teaspoons garam masala

1 tablespoon dried chopped chives

1 tablespoon dried chopped parsley

1 tablespoon dried Italian seasoning

1 teaspoon crushed red pepper

1 tablespoon apple cider vinegar

2 tablespoons balsamic vinegar

½ cup melted butter

1 tablespoon soy sauce

1 tablespoon red hot sauce

2 tablespoons grape jelly

Rub the duck liberally with salt and wash it under water. Pat it dry with paper towels. Take a knife and score it crisscross on the skin. This is done so that the excess fat drips out of it. On a cookie sheet lined with aluminum foil (for quick cleanup), rest the duck on a baker's rack. This is to ensure that excess fat is collected in the cookie sheet and can be stored or discarded. Using your hands (I prefer to wear gloves), mix all the ingredients together and then *proceed to rub it into the flesh of the duck. Make sure that even the stomach cavity is nicely coated with the marinade. Heat the oven to 350° and place the duck on the center rack of the oven. Set your timer for one hour.*

In the meantime, cook the potatoes in salted water for about 10 minutes, then drain and keep them aside. After the duck has roasted for an hour, remove it from the oven and turn it on the other side. Place the boiled potatoes, already coated in the marinade, around the duck and put it back in the oven. Again continue roasting for another half hour at the end of which, take out the duck once more and turn it to the other side. Put it back in for another half hour after which the duck will be ready. The duck is cooked altogether for two hours. Then it is time to place it on a beautiful platter surrounded by the potatoes for your guests to admire and relish!

7

Club Cook's Fish Pie

The company that dad worked for was situated in a small village called Koratty. It comprised of a good-sized mill and housing, all within the walled confines of a sixty-acre compound. The officers' quarters were at one end of the compound, and the foremen's quarters were at the other end. Altogether, this was home for about four hundred people at any given time. In the officers' quarters, which was made up of beautiful homes with gardens, there were people from all over India, and even the world. We grew up with friends whose families came from as far away as Brazil and Scotland, and even among the Indians there were people who came from places as diverse as northern Punjab and Bangladesh. We were a multinational, multiethnic, multicultural lot, and this made things all the more interesting. In order to keep everyone going, there were a whole lot of parties. The central hub of social life was the clubhouse that organized parties every month and usually with different themes like Arabian Nights, English Pubs, Casino Night, and so on. For Arabian Nights, the whole club would be decked out with bolster cushions with everyone sitting on them eating kebabs. Casino Night would involve card tables and other fun. Life was exciting and there was never a dull moment. Some of the parties would take place around the big pool and, being in the tropics, nobody thought anything of pushing a few people into the pool at the end of the party!

The individual officers used to have their own annual house parties. While my mother prepared for a party with a mixture of anxiety and excitement, my father, ever the extrovert, looked forward to these events with a lot of anticipation. He was always the genial host and knew how to show his guests a good time. My father would set up his bar like a tiki hut and would offer the ladies different concoctions to sample! As for us kids, it was tremendous excitement, although we were not allowed to participate in the party. We were the balcony observers, and along with our nanny, we watched the whole event unfold by hiding behind the balcony rail. We would see ladies dressed up in beautiful colorful saris, the North Indian ladies in their beautiful gossamer thin chiffons, and the South Indian ladies in their beautiful Kancheevaram silks with their gold borders. The smell of perfume would be in the air. Amid the men's manly voices and loud laughter, you could occasionally hear the tinkling laughter of the ladies. It was all so exciting! The appetizers and the drinks would be passed around by bearers in uniforms, and later there would be dinner and dessert and after dinner drinks.

My mother would always be in a state of nervous anxiety on the day of the party. She would be waiting in anticipation for the club cook's arrival because this was an occasion that demanded more than her normal repertoire of cooking. She would have seen to most of the appetizers and many of the main courses, but she would insist on calling the club cook to make a special dish that appealed to our English guests. The club cook would arrive wearing his chef's whites and looking very self-important. My mother would be running through the ingredients with him. He would then proceed to make the dish with my mother wringing her hands by his side, hoping it got done on time. I used to think that maybe it was something very difficult to do because my mother did not trust herself to do it. Only much later did I realize that it may actually have been simpler than many of the dishes that we made regularly. She was fretting more because it was an unfamiliar western dish that she did not make often. We kids got to taste it only the next day because we were in bed and not allowed to go to the party. But it all tasted wonderful and extraordinary because they were things we did not get on a regular day.

Club Cook's Fish Pie

Ingredients:

2 pounds of white fish flesh (cod, red snapper, tilapia, halibut or swordfish)

2 cups of heavy cream

1 cup of frozen peas and carrots

1 chopped onion

6 pods chopped garlic

salt to taste

2 teaspoons ground black pepper

2 teaspoons garlic powder

1 teaspoon onion powder

1 tablespoon chopped fresh basil

½ teaspoon grated nutmeg

3 tablespoon all-purpose flour

1 teaspoon baking powder

2 beaten eggs

1 packet cream cheese

1 tablespoon chopped fresh chives

1 stick of butter

¼ cup of water

In a saucepan at medium heat, melt the butter and add to it the onions and garlic. When browned, add salt, pepper, garlic powder, onion powder, and the grated nutmeg and combine. At this point, add the all-purpose flour and keep stirring so that it does not burn. Give it a minute to take the raw taste out of the flour. Add the fish, the vegetables, and one fourth of a cup of water and cook covered for about five minutes. When the fish becomes flakey, add the heavy cream, softened cream cheese, chives, beaten eggs, and baking powder and transfer the whole mixture into a casserole dish sprayed with Pam. Bake in a preheated 350-degree oven for about half an hour or until the top starts to brown slightly. It will make for a delightful casserole!

8

Mary's Beef and Plantain Curry

Trichur was our ancestral home and where my paternal grandmother lived. My father's mother was quite the matriarch living in this huge, grand old home. Her husband, my grandfather, was the secretary of state for the maharaja of Cochin. Ammamma, as we called her, was not someone to be taken lightly! Tall and patrician looking, she had raised seven sons and four daughters. Her sons were all highly placed and even at age eighty-six, she could tell you their exact designations. She was a highly intelligent, no nonsense person who did not suffer fools gladly. As a young girl she had to give up her education even though she was a scholarship student because her mother died prematurely and left her to care for a six-month-old brother.

Summers spent in the Trichur house were pure magic. Once our car pulled into the sloping wide driveway down to the main compound, it was utter lawlessness. Every summer all my uncles and aunts along with their numerous kids would come to spend the summer in the family home. We kids waited with such anticipation to get there while our mother dreaded it because she felt she had no control over us. Girls and boys alike climbed the many trees in the compound—mango, guava, and even palm trees were fair game. We swung from the branches like little monkeys and in the process sometimes suffered injuries which today would have meant an emergency room visit, but in those days was just something that you hid from your parents for fear of punishment. We used to run down the banks into the shallow pond that was full of little minnow fishes. Then one of our older cousins would play a prank and yell at the top of his voice, "Snake, I see a snake slithering in the water!" which was enough to provoke a mad scramble of younger cousins screaming and crying as they ran out of the water! Beyond the thorny fence that demarcated our boundary, there were rice paddy fields. So of course we had to jump down the fence and go and play cricket in someone else's rice paddy fields. There would be another mad scramble up the fence when an indignant farmer chased us out of his fields. We would dare each other to shimmy up the single trunk of a mango tree that grew from the garden and went up two stories high to street-level, branching out on top of my grandfather's garage. The adults engaged in their own entertainment by playing cards, and hence they were too busy to see what we were up to. We would clamber up to the top of the garage and have our own card game. I can't think of a more fun place than my grandmother's house in the summer.

Mealtimes were just as eventful in the Trichur house. Altogether there would be about fifty people. The meals were fairly simple but always tasty, and always followed the same pattern. Kids would be fed first in the dining room at the lower level of the house, followed by the adults, and after that the various servants who had traveled with us; they would have their own private dinner, eating in the kitchen. Ammamma's cook was Mary, about forty-five years of age. My grandmother never believed in micromanaging her cook, and hence Mary became very experienced at managing the kitchen. She bossed all the other servants around, and at dinner times those who were in her favor received extra helpings of the curries. She was a reasonably good cook who could prepare all the country delicacies. There were four meals to be made every day, including something for tea. Ready-made items like cookies and cakes were hardly available because industrial production of them was very sporadic, and the few items that were sold commercially were frightfully expensive.

Beef was a staple in the Kerala Christian diet, more so because the Hindus did not eat it. While it was cheap and plentiful, one should not mistake it for the great Angus beef or the succulent steaks that the Western world feasted on. These cows worked hard all their lives and were slaughtered when they could not work anymore. Their meat was tough and often had to be pressure cooked. Plantains grew in plenty in all our yards and they were often the vegetable that was used with meat in order to stretch the curry.

Mary's Beef and Plantain Curry

Ingredients:

2 pounds of beef stew meat	salt to taste
4 green plantains	3 teaspoons turmeric
3 tablespoons coconut oil	3 teaspoon chili powder
1 chopped onion	4 teaspoon coriander powder
2 tablespoons curry leaves	
1 teaspoon garlic powder	6 cloves of garlic
1 teaspoon ground black pepper	2 green chilies
1 teaspoon onion powder	1 finger length of ginger
	2 cans of coconut milk
2 tablespoons apple cider vinegar	2 cans of water

Chop off the two ends of the plantains and shave off the ridges on them. (Useful tip: it is advisable to wear gloves while handling plantains because they have a sticky, black sap on them). With the skin on, cut them into cubes and put them in a pot with water, a pinch of turmeric and salt, and boil them for 10 minutes until tender. Drain the water and keep the plantains aside. Wash the beef well and put it in a pressure cooker along with salt, 1 teaspoon turmeric, 1 teaspoon chili powder, 1 teaspoon garlic powder, 1 teaspoon ground black pepper, 1 teaspoon onion powder,

2 tablespoons of apple cider vinegar, and one can of water. When the steam appears at the top of the pressure cooker, put the weight on and cook it at medium-high for about 12 minutes. In a blender, grind 2 teaspoons turmeric powder, 2 teaspoons chili powder, 4 teaspoons coriander powder, six cloves of garlic, 2 green chilies, and the ginger. In a saucepan at medium heat, pour in the coconut oil and add the onions and curry leaves to it. When it is a dark shade of brown, add the blender mix and stir it till the raw taste goes out of it. To this add two cans of coconut milk and one can of water. At this time, add the beef and the plantains already cooked to the mixture and cook it for another 10 minutes at medium low until the stew comes to a low boil. It is delicious when served with rice.

9

The Midnight Omelet

My siblings and I loved it when Dad and Mom had to go to a night-time party. Since most of the company parties started at 8:30 (a concession to the heat of the tropics), my mother would serve us dinner before she went up to get ready. She was always suspicious if we seemed too eager for her to leave the house. We loved to watch her dress. The last thing she would do was put on her beautiful jewelry and then dab perfume behind her ears and on her wrists. To us girls it was the culmination of being a grown-up, fancy lady. And then they were off, my father in his jaunty safari suit and my mother trying to keep up with his long strides in her fancy sari and platform heels.

We were left in the company of two sisters who were our nannies. They themselves were only fourteen and seventeen at the time and hence not a lot older than us. They were only too glad to get a break from their everyday chores and join us in our escapades. We lived in two adjoining houses at that time and our neighbor Remani Aunty was very industrious and kept a big henhouse by the side of her home. Her daughter Rohini was good friends with all of us. Every time we passed by her house, we could hear the "buc, buc, buc" of the white leghorns who called the henhouse their home. There was one mean rooster who thought highly of himself and was the king of the castle. Our neighboring house also had an abundance of fruit trees like Ceylon apple and rose apple (Chaambanga as we called it). We helped ourselves liberally to these when Eliachedathy was not looking. Eliachedathy was the housekeeper for the neighboring family. Thin, emaciated, and in her 60s, she was the guardian of their estate. The Hindu girls in our school came adorned with jasmine flowers in their hair, and hence we felt the need to do the same. But my mother only grew roses and so we helped ourselves to Eliachedathy's jasmine flowers as well.

After my parents left for their party, we put our plan in motion. My sister and I left for the henhouse, which was next door. Valsa and Vimala, my mother's trusted assistants, kept a watch outside. The hens had retreated to their sleeping chamber and the eggs they laid were lying scattered around the coop. There was a small tear in the wire surrounding the coop, and using a stick we coaxed the eggs toward the tear and could slowly retrieve them. When we were about to get our second egg the rooster decided at that moment to make a fuss. We hear a door opening and scramble to hide by the side of the chicken coop. It was Eliachedathy coming! She came to the other side and by this time we are wetting our pants in the effort of trying to hold down the giggles. She is talking to herself and cursing the fox she was certain was responsible for sending her rooster into a tizzy. With a reassuring word to her bird man, she went inside again and closed the door. We retrieved four more eggs, bringing up the total to six! Then it was time for a delicious midnight omelet made all the more scrumptious for the labor involved.

The Midnight Omelet

Ingredients:

6 large eggs beaten well

8 shallots, finely chopped

1 green chili, finely chopped

10 curry leaves

salt to taste

½ teaspoon chili powder

4 tablespoons coconut oil

Heat the coconut oil to medium heat in a wok. In a large bowl, beat the eggs well, add the rest of the ingredients, and pour it into the oil. Scramble it at first and then when the bottom of the omelet starts to congeal, flip it onto the other side. Makes for a delicious snack or breakfast and even a midnight snack after a particularly harrowing adventure!

10

Sheefa's Whole Fried Fish
with Mango Sauce

Sheefa is the third child among my parent's five children. Lively and vivacious, she is an inspiring educator to her many pupils. She is also an excellent cook. Her husband's family lived in Malaysia because his father had gone to work there as an engineer. His mother was brought up in Malaysia just like my brother-in-law and his siblings. The family settled in India only when the children came of age and were ready to go to college. Then it was decided that in order for them to learn Indian culture, it was better that they come back to India. They developed a fondness for the local cuisine of Malaysia with its mix of Chinese, Thai, Indian, Korean, and Vietnamese flavors. Even today, if you asked many Indians what their favorite food is apart from Indian food, they will say it is Chinese. There were many Chinese immigrants who settled in the bigger cities of India, and they brought with them their cuisine and adapted it to the Indian taste. In Indian Chinese, you will find ingredients such as green chilies and even coriander leaves. One of the other professions that is predominated by Asians in India is hairstyling. Many beauty parlors are started by Chinese immigrants.

This is a dish that is inspired by Indian and Asian flavors. The fried fish has all the usual ingredients of a Kerala fish fry, while the sauce is a mix of Oriental and Indian ingredients. The first time Sheefa served this to us was during one of our family gatherings. Everyone was impressed and we really did justice to the dish! If I remember right, she had fried a whole tilapia. The presentation is very impressive too. For those who do not wish to handle a whole fish with bones included, you can substitute a whole fish fillet or even pieces of fish.

Sheefa's Whole Fried Fish with Mango Sauce

Ingredients:

1 whole fish dressed, scaled and gutted, the inside gills taken out with only the cover remaining. (The eyes can be left intact or taken out and replaced with cherry tomatoes after frying.) Suitable fish varieties include tilapia, red snapper, grouper, trout, or any kind of flat fish that fries evenly crispy.

Salt to taste

2 teaspoons turmeric powder

2 teaspoons chili powder

2 teaspoons coriander powder

2 teaspoons garlic powder

2 teaspoon ground black pepper

1 teaspoon onion powder

2 teaspoons ginger powder

2 tablespoons apple cider vinegar

3 cups vegetable oil

Take the cleaned fish, and with a sharp knife score the flesh three times on both sides. This enables the spices to get deep into the body of the fish. Mix the spices well and, with gloves on, rub it liberally on the fish inside and out. Leave it to marinate for one hour. Heat the oil in a shallow saucepan till medium high and gently slide in the fish. Cook for about five minutes on one side and then turn it to the other side and repeat cooking for another five minutes. If the oil becomes too hot, turn the heat down and

43

continue with the process. Be careful while turning the fish, and use wide spatulas so that the oil does not burn you. When the fish is done, place it on a platter lined with paper towels.

Mango Sauce Ingredients:

1 can of Alphonso mango pulp

¼ cup coconut oil

2 tablespoons black mustard seeds

6 dry chili pods

1 chopped onion

6 cloves chopped garlic

1 chopped green chilies

1 finger length chopped ginger

2 tablespoons chopped coriander leaves

2 tablespoons curry leaves

Salt to taste

2 teaspoons garam masala powder

2 teaspoons garlic powder

2 teaspoons ground black pepper

1 teaspoon onion powder

1 tablespoon dried chopped parsley

1 tablespoon dried chopped chives

1 tablespoon Italian seasoning

1 teaspoon crushed chili powder

3 tablespoons balsamic vinegar

6 tablespoons soy sauce

2 teaspoons hot sauce (something like Tabasco)

1 tablespoon sugar

1 tablespoon cornstarch

1 can of coconut milk

3 cups of water

2 tablespoons apple cider vinegar

In a saucepan at medium heat, pour in the coconut oil, and when the oil gets hot, add the mustard seeds and the dry chili pods. When the mustard starts to pop, add in the chopped onion, chopped garlic, chopped green chilies, chopped ginger, chopped cilantro, and the curry leaves. Sauté until the onions become translucent and add the salt, garam masala, garlic powder, onion powder, ground black pepper, chives, parsley, Italian seasoning, and the crushed chili powder. Stir for a minute and then add balsamic vinegar, apple cider vinegar, soy sauce, and the red hot sauce. To this add the mango pulp and the coconut milk. In a bowl, make a slurry with the cornstarch and water and add this as well. Add the sugar to the mixture and stir until everything is well incorporated. Cook it on medium-low until it reaches a rolling boil. Pour it over the fish in a flat platter and serve. It can be served with noodles or rice.

11

Deepa's Chicken Biriyani

*D**eepa, my second sister,** is married to a lawyer. His family comes from a very picturesque region in the south of Kerala. With its rolling hills and lush vegetation, it is extremely fertile land. India has been known even from ancient days for its spices and silk. Traders from Europe, Africa, and the Middle East came regularly to load up their ships with what they used to call "black gold." Pepper was more valuable than gold in the ancient world. Pepper plants climb like little serpents on the big trees, and when it is time to harvest, you can see the numerous little stocks with its pearls of pepper studded on them. Star anise, cardamom, and cinnamon stalks grow in plenty around this region. Mangusteen, a delightfully fleshy fruit, as well as several varieties of bananas, grow in profusion around here. There are rubber plantations everywhere, and during harvest time, you can see the rubber tappers with their buckets making a groove on the tree and hanging their buckets at the bottom of the cut on the bark in order to catch the resin. The resin is then processed and made into sheets of rubber which fetch quite a price in the world markets. Given the abundance of spices growing there, it is only natural that they used more of them in their food.

Biriyani, or "Biryani" as it is sometimes called by the rest of the world, has its origins in the Middle East. Even in the chronicles of the Mughal Empire, they talk about Emperor Humayoon enjoying a dish of aromatic rice cooked with delicately spiced lamb. India was occupied by the Muslims for close to a thousand years, and we have adopted many aspects of their food culture. Biriyani is still one of the most enjoyed dishes in India. When I was a young girl in India, when we talked about going out to eat it was always for a plate of Biriyani garnished with the quintessential fried onions and a boiled egg on top. In our house, Deepa was the biryani maker. My mother would always call on her expertise whenever guests came and biryani had to be made.

Deepa's Chicken Biriyani

Ingredients:

12 chicken thighs washed well

Salt to taste

2 teaspoons turmeric powder

2 teaspoons chili powder

2 teaspoons ground black pepper

2 teaspoons garlic powder

1 teaspoon onion powder

2 tablespoons apple cider vinegar

1 cup of water

Place the chicken and all the ingredients into a pressure cooker and mix them well. Close the lid, set it to high heat, and when the pressure starts to escape, put on the weight and lower the heat to medium-high. Let it cook for ten to twelve minutes; it should be tender.

Ingredients for the biriyani:

3 cups of basmati rice washed and rinsed

1 cup onion, chopped

6 cloves of garlic, chopped

4 green chilies, chopped

1 finger length ginger, peeled and chopped

3 tablespoons cilantro chopped

3 tablespoons curry leaves

Salt to taste

1 teaspoon turmeric powder

2 teaspoons chili powder

2 teaspoons garam masala

2 teaspoons ground black pepper

2 teaspoons garlic powder

1 teaspoon onion powder

½ teaspoon methi (fenugreek) powder

4 star anise flowers

2 teaspoons black cumin seeds

3 sticks of cinnamon

6 cardamom pods

6 pieces of cloves

6 dried bay leaves

1 piece of mace (outer cover of the nutmeg)

1 cup of sour cream

2 tablespoons apple cider vinegar

2 cups of water

¼ cup of vegetable oil

3 sticks of butter

In a large pot with a tight lid, spray the bottom and sides of the pot thoroughly with Pam. Heat it to medium-high and pour in the oil. Add three sticks of butter to it along with the onions, garlic, green chilies, ginger, coriander leaves, and the curry leaves. Also add the star anise, cumin seeds, cardamom, cinnamon sticks, cloves, mace, and the bay leaves (leave these spices whole and not powdered). When the mixture is slightly brown, add salt, turmeric, chili powder, garam masala, garlic powder, black pepper, onion powder, and methi. After a minute stir in the sour cream, apple cider vinegar, and water. Empty out the contents of the pressure cooker into the pot and mix everything well. Close the lid and cook it for about five minutes until small bubbles start coming up in the liquid. This is the time to add your rice and stir it again. Close the lid and lower the temperature to medium low and cook for 15 minutes. After 5 minutes, lift the lid and give it a good stir, making sure no rice sticks to the bottom. Close the lid and continue cooking for the rest of the time at very low heat. After 15 minutes, open the lid and pour out the rice and chicken mixture into a deep, rectangular pan that has been thoroughly sprayed with Pam. Spread it out evenly and close it tightly with aluminum foil. Put it in a preheated 350° oven for 15 minutes. Your biriyani is almost ready. Now all that remains is the garnish and the boiled eggs.

Ingredients for garnish:

One onion sliced

6 eggs, boiled for 20 minutes in water

1 stick of butter

¼ cup raisins

½ cup cashews

In a shallow saucepan, melt one stick of butter and add the sliced onions. Stir the onions at medium heat until they turn fairly brown. Then add a pinch of salt plus the cashews and raisins and garnish your biriyani with this mixture. Arrange the shelled boiled eggs artfully on top. If the visuals alone don't get you, the aromatic smell definitely will make you long for a plate of this delicacy!

12

Raphael's Favorite Samosas

Raphael is the fourth among my siblings. He is a man of the world. An accomplished dentist, he has two dental clinics in Bangalore. He is also an avid golfer and a keen tennis player. He has the energy of a much younger man and puts the rest of us to shame for not being as fit as he is! He eats at the best restaurants and is always first in line to try out a new place that shows some promise. Raphael has inside knowledge about the Bangalore dining scene and he counts many of the finest chefs in Bangalore as his best friends. He and his wife are very careful about where they eat and what they eat. But there is one indulgence that is so scrumptious that my brother does not care that it does not come from a five-star restaurant: the samosas made by the little Muslim shop around the corner. You can see the little cook with his white cap casually adding uncooked samosas to the huge iron wok bubbling with oil. And, presto! The crunchy pastries with their spicy filling of lamb, potatoes, and sautéed onions come out so golden delicious. It is the unmistakable smell of indulgence, pure and simple. When the siblings gather together in my father's flat, Raphael will bound in brandishing a brown paper bag dotted with little circles of grease. The smell of samosas is overpowering and everyone jumps up to grab one!

Every culture has its variation of vegetable or meat pastries. Samosas can be vegetarian or non-vegetarian depending on the crowd. It can be an appetizer, snack, or a tea-time favorite and hence it has become an international dish. The following recipe can be made vegetarian or non-vegetarian. The purists will argue that the pastry part of the Samosa has to be made from all-purpose flour, salt, and water. I do not believe that cooking has to be complicated, and I feel that it is perfectly all right to use either tortilla or egg roll wrappers as a substitute. Egg roll wrappers are prone to absorb more oil and hence I prefer to use the flat, flour tortillas.

Raphael's Favorite Samosas

Ingredients:

6 medium flour tortillas

6 potatoes, peeled and cubed

1 onion, sliced thin

6 cloves of garlic, chopped

4 green chilies, chopped

1 finger length of ginger, chopped

2 teaspoons garam masala powder

2 tablespoons chopped coriander leaves

2 tablespoons curry leaves

Salt to taste

1 teaspoon turmeric powder

1 teaspoon chili powder

2 teaspoons garlic powder

2 teaspoons ground black pepper

1 teaspoon onion powder

½ teaspoon of methi (fenugreek powder)

½ cup of frozen peas

2 tablespoons all-purpose flour

3 tablespoons coconut oil

3 cups of vegetable oil for frying

Place the cubed potatoes in a pot with water and salt and cook for 15 minutes until tender. Then drain out the water and mash with a potato masher. Pour the coconut oil into a shallow saucepan heated to medium high and add the onions, garlic, chilis, ginger, coriander leaves, curry leaves, and salt. Next, add the frozen peas and stir again. When the mixture becomes translucent, add the turmeric powder, chili powder, garlic powder, black pepper, onion powder, and the methi (fenugreek) powder. To this mixture add the mashed potatoes and incorporate thoroughly. Keep it aside to cool a little.

In a small bowl make an "edible glue" of 2 tablespoons of all-purpose flour and 1 tablespoon of water mixed together. Take a flour tortilla and place it in the microwave for 25 seconds. Take it out and cut it in half. Spoon a ball of the potato mixture onto the lower half of the divided tortilla. Apply the edible glue liberally on the sides. Then bring the top flap to cover the potatoes and pinch it tightly at the edges so that the whole thing is a sealed triangle. Hint: make sure the edges are tight or it will splatter when put in oil.

In a wok, pour in the vegetable oil and heat it to 350 degrees or about medium high. Do not burn the oil. Slide in your samosas and fry on both sides until golden brown, then remove them from the wok with a slotted spoon and place them on a platter lined with paper towels.

Meat Samosas:
Ingredients:

2 pounds of ground lamb or beef	2 cups of the potato mixture made according to the recipe for the vegetable samosas

Proceed to brown the lamb or beef in a saucepan and when cooked, drain out the excess fat and add the potato mixture that we prepared for the vegetarian samosas. Mix thoroughly and make samosas with the half tortilla as specified for the vegetarian samosas. Frying is also done the same way.

Whether meat or vegetarian, samosas can be eaten with green cilantro chutney, sweet date chutney, or just plain ketchup.

13

The Birthday Party Cheese Toast

We *were the Enid Blyton children.* All of us had read every book ever written by Enid Blyton, and we tried to mimic the actions of our young heroes. They were all about a couple of young kids who solved the mysteries that were plaguing their neighborhood. They did not involve murder or mayhem but were centered round things like, "Who stole the bicycle?" Or, "Who stole the neighbor's paper?" or something equally mundane. There was always the ineffectual bobby (as the police were referred to in England) who was spinning his wheels and unable to solve the mystery even with all the authority available to him. Then there would be the secret seven, the group of young people aged ten to thirteen who would run around gathering clue after clue and in the end would triumphantly solve the mystery. We were so enthralled by their adventures. It was from them that we learned the art of passing secret messages by writing them on paper with orange juice, and the receiver would decode it by ironing the paper. It was the stuff of Sherlock Holmes. We had our own secret societies, and we even had rival secret societies where we would leave notes written in orange juice at the appropriate destinations only to have our counterpart ironing furiously at home to decode a message which would read something like, "Tina loves John!"

Birthday parties were a lot of fun. All the neighborhood kids would be invited and they would come wearing their party dresses. The presents were not as expensive as the gifts exchanged now. They would usually consist of pens, special writing stationary, a dress material, or even sometimes a fancy pair of sandals. They were simply wrapped and tied with a few ribbons. Mommy would make cheese toast, banana fritters, Jell-O, and egg sandwiches, and the choice of beverage was always squash (we called any juice "squash" whether it was orange or lime). After tea would come the games. These were also inspired by the children's authors of those days. We had treasure hunts, word games, charades, and some athletic games like a small team relay race. The winners would be presented small chocolate bars or a fancy pen. This was followed by Daddy's magic show. By the time we were all grown up, he had gotten quite good at it and he could make things disappear in a hat or make two plastic dolls seem to dance in thin air. He had bought the supplies for this show and only later did we realize that there was a gossamer thin thread connecting the dolls to the opposite wall and the other end of the seemingly invisible thread was in his hand. The take away gifts were equally modest. Mom would have made little pouches of wrapped candy, colored pencils, erasers, and maybe a handkerchief. We thoroughly looked forward to a birthday party!

The Birthday Party Cheese Toast

Ingredients:

10 slices of any hardy bread, with each slice cut into four

8 eggs well beaten

Half an onion, well chopped

1 green chili, well chopped

1 tablespoon curry leaves chopped

1 cup grated sharp cheddar cheese

3 tablespoons all-purpose flour

2 teaspoons baking powder

Salt to taste

1 teaspoon ground black pepper

½ teaspoon chili powder

2 cups of vegetable oil for frying

Beat the eggs well in a bowl and add the rest of the ingredients. Mix thoroughly. Take one of the little cut square pieces of bread and place a spoonful of batter in the center of it. Pour the oil into a shallow saucepan and heat it to medium high. When the oil reaches about 350°, place the square pieces of bread with the batter side down into the oil. Make sure that you place it with the batter side down in the oil. Do not attempt to flip it because the plain bread side would absorb too much oil. Hence it's cooked only on one side. In about three minutes the squares can be taken out of the oil and placed in a platter lined with paper towels. These are so delicious, and if you want to get fancier, you can add sausage, ham, or bell peppers to the mixture. It can also be served as an appetizer for cocktails.

14

Coconut Plucking Day:
"Kallu" Toddy and Spicy Sardines

addy, along with his brother, Varghese Uncle owned an acre of land close to the Cochin backwaters in a small town called Edappalli. It was mainly a coconut plantation surrounded by sand and rustic country roads. Once every three months it was time to pluck the coconuts and sell them in the markets. Daddy had the unique ability to turn even the most mundane activity into a lot of fun. Coconut plucking was a boring, routine activity in most households but was transformed into a fun picnic by my parents. My four siblings and I along with our parents and the two young nannies would pile into dad's light-chocolate and cream-colored Dodge with its big tailfins. Mom would have her headscarf on, and her job would be to mediate the skirmishes in the backseat.

When we arrived at the compound, the overseer would come running from his hut to greet us, smiling broadly. He was, I am sure, even more glad to see his two daughters, who were our nannies. He was a poor man and his house was a thatched roof hut. He had so many children and was only too glad to send two of them with us so that we would feed them and he could get their wages. Valsa and Vimala, the two girls, would run to the house with excitement and greet their brothers and sisters. Their mother, a shy, tiny little lady, would come out with the latest child on her hip nursing at her saggy, wilted breasts. We got to see inside the hut and, not having a clue as to how hard their life was, it all seemed very romantic.

The overseer was a tall man with a scraggly beard, and when he smiled, it looked like only one side of his mouth had teeth. He would talk to dad differentially and tell him of the state of the plantation while the coconut plucker would be standing aside waiting for his orders to start. He was a short, wiry man with just a loincloth, and his only tools of the trade were loop of ropes and his machete. When he got the okay to start, he would place both his feet inside the looped rope and, machete in hand, would start clambering up the coconut tree, monkey style. He was knowledgeable in his art and could differentiate between the coconuts ready for plucking and the tender ones and could also climb to extraordinary heights! He also knew how to prune the trees after hacking away at the coconuts that needed to come down. We knew not to stand under the tree he was climbing! There were also coconut trees in the compound that were only a little taller than ourselves and produced tender orange coconuts. We tried to climb these trees in imitation of the coconut plucker's art. The coconut plucker would use his machete and shave off the tops of the tender coconuts so that we could enjoy the delicious, sweet water inside. When we were finished drinking, he would split the coconut in half so that we could scoop out the tender flesh. Mom would spread a big sheet under one of the shady trees and Dad would send the overseer to get us Toddy and Spicy Sardine Curry from the nearest toddy (liquor) shop. Toddy, or "Kallu" as it is locally known, is the fermented juice of the coconut tree. While most of us liked the slightly fermented sweet variety, the hard-core drunkards would go for the highly fermented, almost sour toddy, which would come from the shop in milk bottles with no caps on. Our grandmother frowned upon my father letting us enjoy a little bit of kallu every now and then, but he did not see any harm in it. In Kerala, a spicy tidbit is a must with any kind of liquor. The men usually take a swig of the drink and then, with their fingers, take a piece of the spicy appetizer and pop it in their mouth. This is supposed to give them a kick. The usual appetizers, or "touchings" as they are affectionately called in Kerala, are spicy fried or curried fish, spicy shrimp, Masala boiled eggs, or chicken wings.

Toddy (Kallu)

Ingredients:

6 cans of coconut water

2 teaspoons active dry
bread yeast

1 cup of sugar

½ cup water

Dissolve the yeast in half a cup of lukewarm water and mix it with the coconut water and the sugar. Keep it in a warm place for about 24 hours. The liquid will look a little milky and will be slightly fermented and sweet. If you would like it more fermented, keep it for some more time and the alcohol content will be higher.

Spicy Sardine Curry
Ingredients:

12 fresh sardines scaled and gutted (you may also use canned sardines, but put less salt in the curry)

Salt to taste

1 large onion, sliced

4 large green chilies, sliced

6 cloves of garlic crushed

One finger length of ginger, peeled and crushed

2 tablespoons curry leaves

6 teaspoons chili powder

2 teaspoons turmeric powder

4 teaspoons coriander powder

6 pieces of kokum (a dried fruit that is black in color and gives the dish its sourness)

1 tablespoon of black mustard seeds

6 dried chili pods

1 cup of water

4 tablespoons coconut oil

In a cup of water, put your washed kokum pieces. Place the cup in the microwave and heat it for about a minute. In a saucepan heated to medium-high, pour in the coconut oil, and when the oil gets hot, add your mustard seeds, the dried chili pods, and the curry leaves. When the mustard starts popping, add the onion, garlic, green chilies, and ginger, and sauté them until they turn brown. At this time, add the turmeric, chili, coriander, and salt, and sauté this mixture for a minute. Add the sardines and the water with the kokum, stir well and cover the pot. The sardines will be cooked and the sauce will be thickened in about 10 minutes at medium heat.

If you find it hard to get kokum (which is available in most Indian stores), you can always substitute tamarind, crushed tomatoes, or green, tart mangoes.

15

Harvest Time:
A Laborer's Breadfruit Breakfast

When my maternal grandfather died at the age of sixty-two of colon cancer, he was at the peak of his career as a lawyer. My grandmother had to leave the city of Madras (Chennai) and all her socialite friends and return to the ancestral home of my grandfather. It was a house that he had inherited and was at least three hundred years old! The ceiling was so low that my father, who was only five feet, ten-and-a-half inches in height would regularly bump his head. The windows were like the portholes of a ship and the wooden shutters were at least ten inches thick. But the woodwork in the house was phenomenal. It had a false ceiling made entirely of teak which kept the house very cool in the blasting summers of Kerala. The well was adjoined to the house since the house had no running water. Electricity came to the village only in 1974. The bathroom was an outhouse and anyone who had the runs at night had to go there in a procession with someone leading the way, illuminating the dense foliage with a kerosene lamp. And the whole time when you are sitting inside the outhouse trying to do the job as quietly as possible, you can hear the debate going on outside as to the root cause of your stomach upheaval. "Ah chakka valiche vaari thinnappazhe njaan vichaarichathaa, vayare mosham aavumnne."("When I saw her stuffing her face with that jackfruit itself, I knew she was going to have stomach issues.") The village outside was privy to the levels of distress going on inside, and the running commentary continues,"nalla vayarilakkam aanenna thonnane"("I think it is a bad case of diarrhea"), as if that was not obvious! The flora and fauna hid many a creature including poisonous cobras and vipers. It was an agricultural estate with the primary crops being rice and coconut.

My grandmother had no idea about farming other than the fact that her folks also owned some rice fields. She was a magistrate's daughter who was more interested in her clothes and jewelry and could not care less when it was harvest time. But all this changed with her move to the village of Mattom, when my grandfather's old ancestral home became her new home. To her credit, she was a fast learner, and together with her able overseer Pallikkutty, she was able to continue farming. Pallikkutty looked like a scaled down version of Arnold Schwarzenegger and he was dedicated to her. He and his wife (who also worked in my grandmother's kitchen) belonged to the mountain tribes who lived in their little huts on a hill beyond the house. The women did not wear blouses and would sometimes cover their breasts with a small thin cloth. Their culture was very unique. When they came face to face with the master of the house, in order to show respect, they would immediately remove the small piece of cloth that covered their breasts, leaving most normal people highly embarrassed! Pallikkutty's wife Kaali was my grandmother's cook-cum-maid. Tall and slender, her hair tied into a topknot, Kaali could have passed for any model on the Paris runway. The only problem was that her teeth were terribly stained from the betel leaves and the areca nuts that she constantly chewed.

Harvest time for rice was a special occasion. The house was specially designed for it. There was a spacious central courtyard that would be sterilized by paving it with fresh cow dung and letting it bake in the sun. In the morning, Pallikkutty would marshal his troops—about fifteen laborers, both men and women. With their scythes, they would cut the stocks bearing the golden grains and bundle it neatly. The women would return from the fields bearing the bundles on their heads, and they would all be collected in the central courtyard. Since the only transportation was by foot, it would take them all day long, and by sunset, the stalks would all have been collected. Then it was time to separate the grain from the stalk. The central courtyard had covered porches on three sides of it with pillars to hold up the roof. Each worker would hold on to the banister rail and, with their feet, work on the bundle almost like a rhythmic dance and separate the paddy grain from the stock. This treading went on all night long in the light of Petromax lanterns since there were no electric lights. Under the watchful eye of the overseer, and helping themselves to ladles of strong, black coffee sweetened with jaggery, they worked on. Lying in a room that adjoined the veranda, I could hear them talking, singing, and sometimes flirting to get through the arduous task. I could hear Kuttan saying, "Kalyani nee cheruppai varaanallo" ("Kalyani, you are looking younger and younger") to which Kalyani, who was more than a little flattered, would reply, "Thaan podo manushyaa, priyam parayanu" ("Get lost man, stop flirting!").

Their eating habits were equally simple. A diet rich in carbohydrates gave them the energy to work in the fields. Breadfruit grew in abundance and it was more available than potato, which had to be bought at the store. When the breadfruit tree was full of fruit, it appeared in some form in just about every dish. We kids would start to grumble that we had had enough of it. Today, I long for a fresh breadfruit and often have to settle for the refrigerated variety found in Asian stores. The worker's meal would often consist of a rice porridge and a breadfruit stir-fry. Even their dining vessels were makeshift. They would take small husks from the coconut tree and make them into a kind of trough by tying both ends with rough vines. The soupy rice and the curry would go into this and they would make a spoon of jack fruit leaves (jack fruit leaves are broad like the magnolia leaves), the end of which would be made into a funnel with a broomstick to hold it in place.

After their meal, they would start the laborious process of boiling the rice husks in a big cauldron. The cauldron was set on a stove made of three huge bricks with firewood burning under it. These were then dried in the courtyard and stored in the upstairs rooms that served as granaries. From these grains, the rice that is commonly eaten in Kerala—a hardy, unpolished rice known as "puzhungiya ari"(boiled rice)—is milled. For all their troubles, the laborers were paid in kind, each laborer going home with about six months' supply of paddy.

A Laborer's Breadfruit Breakfast

Ingredients:

2 green breadfruits

10 shallots. finely chopped

Six cloves of garlic, finely chopped

2 green chilies, finely chopped

2 tablespoons curry leaves

Salt to taste

2 teaspoons turmeric powder

2 teaspoons chili powder

3 tablespoons coconut oil

Remove the green skin of the breadfruit and cut it into two. Then cut each half into two pieces. Remove the center core from each of the pieces. Cut each piece into thinner wedges. Each of these thin slices can then be horizontally cut so that they look like little triangles. Boil it with water and salt for about 10 minutes or until it becomes tender like a potato. Drain the water and keep it aside. In a skillet heated to medium-high, pour the coconut oil and add the shallots, garlic, green chilies, and curry leaves. Stir it till it starts to brown and then add the salt, turmeric, and chili powder. Now add the breadfruit and mix gently so as not to break up all the pieces of breadfruit. For those who have eaten it, the breadfruit is any day a lot more flavorful than a potato.

Raw breadfruit can also be cut into thin triangles and deep fried in oil to make some wonderful chips for snacking!

16

Mummy's Monday Ladies' Tea Sandwiches

Monday late afternoon around 4:30 is when the ladies of the Koratty compound got together at the clubhouse for their weekly tea. The wives of the officers had very little dealings outside of the compound. The grocery shopping was done mainly by the help. Once a month the company car would take them to Cochin, where they could shop for fabric since most clothes in India in those days were made by tailors. They might go to visit relatives with their family, and that was the extent of their sojourns outside. So they really looked forward to the ladies' tea on Monday afternoons. The circle would include about thirty ladies who would meet in the anteroom of the clubhouse with its colorful seats and cushions along the wall. This was their chance to show off the latest casual styles in saris and salwaar kammeezes. I remember my mother always carrying a handkerchief when she went outside the house. These were the days when paper tissues were unknown to most in the developing world. Being industrious housewives, many women carried their knitting, crochet, embroidery, or cross-stitching and worked on it while chatting at tea.

Two women were always in charge of the snacks for the tea. One made the sweet item, and the other made the savory one. They would call each other on the telephone during weekdays and coordinate their efforts. They took a lot of pride in this effort. On the day of the tea, a club bearer in his white uniform would come to our house to pick up the item that my mother was assigned to make and take it to the club house. After all the ladies had gathered together, the club staff would present the dishes, along with the tea that had been made in the club. My mother, in other words, did not have to carry her dish to the party like all of us are now obliged to do when we have to go for a potluck.

I assume they talked about the children's education (this is the part that we dreaded, because many a tall tale about school would be discovered), the fashions of the day, a smattering of politics, new recipes, and other such topics that were in the realm of housewives in those days. If anyone had a particular topic of interest that they wanted to enlighten the others about, they would then proceed to do so. Sometimes the English ladies would regale their Indian counterparts with the current hot topics in England. Whenever we kids would enter the clubhouse to play table tennis, we could hear the noisy conversations going on and the occasional laughter. They all seemed to have a very good time and my mother thoroughly enjoyed herself. She usually came back with copies of *Ladies' Home Journal* or *Good Housekeeping*. I guess it was a real housewives' convention!

Mummy's Monday Ladies' Tea Sandwiches

Mint Chutney Sandwich

Ingredients:

6 slices of white bread

1 stick of fresh churned butter

2 bunches of mint leaves

½ onion quartered

2 green chilies

1 finger length of ginger, peeled

6 tablespoons apple cider vinegar

Salt to taste

¼ cup of cashew nuts

1 tablespoon ground black pepper

In a blender, grind together the mint leaves, onion, chilies, ginger, apple cider vinegar, salt, cashew nuts, and the black pepper. This is your mint chutney. Take 2 slices of the bread, apply the butter liberally and spread two tablespoons of the chutney on one slice. Cover it with the other slice of bread, cut off the crusts, and make it into 4 small square sandwiches or 2 triangular sandwiches.

Tomato Sandwiches

Ingredients:

6 slices of challah bread

2 tomatoes, sliced

1 cucumber, peeled and sliced

Mayonnaise

Amul cheese slices (you can also use fresh mozzarella, Swiss, or Gouda)

Salt to taste

Ground black pepper

Take 2 pieces of challah bread, and apply mayonnaise to them. Place the sliced tomatoes and cucumbers along with the cheese on one side of the bread. Sprinkle it liberally with salt and black pepper, cut the crusts off and serve it as sandwich wedges.

Egg Sandwiches

Ingredients:

Six eggs boiled for 20 minutes and cooled

¼ cup mayonnaise

¼ cup smoked salmon chopped

3 shallots, finely chopped

1 teaspoon ground black pepper

Salt to taste

½ teaspoon paprika powder

1 teaspoon of peppercorns

1 tablespoon ranch dressing

In a bowl, mash the shelled eggs, but don't make it into a pulp. You need some texture to the eggs. To this add the mayonnaise, salmon, shallots, ground black pepper, salt, paprika, peppercorns, and the ranch dressing. Mix it well and spread it liberally on one side of the bread. Cover it with another slice and remove the crusts. The classic egg sandwich presentation is a triangle.

The sandwiches can be arranged on a platter like my mother used to or you can display it on the old-fashioned tiered tray.

17

A Tiffin Carrier Lunch: Beef Olathe

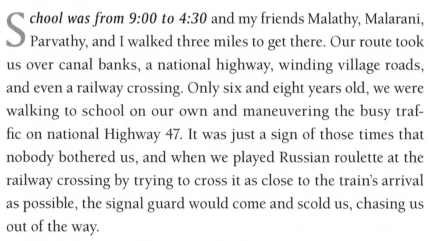

School was from 9:00 to 4:30 and my friends Malathy, Malarani, Parvathy, and I walked three miles to get there. Our route took us over canal banks, a national highway, winding village roads, and even a railway crossing. Only six and eight years old, we were walking to school on our own and maneuvering the busy traffic on national Highway 47. It was just a sign of those times that nobody bothered us, and when we played Russian roulette at the railway crossing by trying to cross it as close to the train's arrival as possible, the signal guard would come and scold us, chasing us out of the way.

We went to a small convent school with open classrooms separated only by screens. The noise from the other classrooms did not bother us and in fact if somebody was being punished with a cane in the other classroom, you can guess where our undivided attention was directed to. Many of my memories after half a century are vague. But I can still remember the tall, fair girl with slightly brown hair and extraordinary blue eyes called Leela. She always looked troubled and kept to herself. One day when we were in the third grade, someone came to the door of the classroom and asked for the nun. She went outside and there were a lot of whisperings after which she came back into the room and told Leela that she was free to go home. Later on, we heard that Leela's mother had committed suicide by jumping into a well. As a young child, I remember being horrified that Leela did not have a mother anymore. She never came back to school.

Even in those days, many of our poorer schools got school lunch aid from Western countries, especially America. This was prepared in the school kitchen, a brick structure with wide open sides covered by a few wooden planks to let out the smoke. The lady in charge of cooking would use the donated wheat flour to make Uppuma, and she would make a big vat of milk using the milk powder that was sent from abroad. The poorest kids were happy enough to get something to eat. Our lunches were sent from home by my mother and were brought to school by our kitchen help. The kids who had the hardest time were the ones whose families were not poor enough and yet not affluent enough to afford to send them lunch. Some of them swallowed their pride and queued up for the school lunch. I still remember this one little girl with curly hair and big eyes; she looked so thin that even a tiny wind would have blown her away, and she always went for a walk in the grounds at lunchtime claiming she was not hungry. She would say that the uppuma gave her a bellyache. Curious George that I was, I wanted to try the uppuma for myself. I always liked wheat products and I thought the uppuma was delicious! So we made a deal. My lunch from home was big enough for two of them and the little girl and her friend, who was also in similar straits, enjoyed it while I enjoyed the uppuma. I did not realize then, but I do now, that it broke a certain barrier, and my parents never chided me for it.

My mother always took pains to balance our nutrition. Lunch was sent in what is called a tiffin carrier. It has four tiers of vessels stacked one on top of the other with a bracket held together with a spoon. Since my sister Deepa and I were in school together, the tiffin carrier would have two vessels of rice, one for each of us, one vessel containing a non-vegetarian dish, and the other one a vegetable. Sometimes there would be a desert or a banana to follow the meal. Deepa and I ate out of our respective rice containers and would help ourselves to the curries with the spoon. There would be a bottle of water used to drink as well as to wash our hands before and after the meal. Indians go for major gargling after a meal in order to cleanse the mouth properly. Josie was the man servant in the house who did all the odd jobs and he was the one who would bring us our lunch. He came from the hills of South Kerala. He came as a scrawny boy and after two years with my mother, he was starting to look plump. He whined to my father that his feet were blistering from walking to school with our lunches, so my father bought him a pair of rubber sandals. He selected his favorite color and he was so proud of them and didn't want to spoil them that he would come bearing our tiffin carrier in one hand, and his sandals in the other, and in his voice like a loud speaker would announce grandly for everyone to hear, "Priya, innu nalla meen varuthathaa!" ("Priya, it's good fish fry today!") which was not at all cool!

During the last year of my school (we finish tenth grade at the age of fifteen and go on to college), the nuns had built a classroom on top of the office room where the principal sat. The corridor from the administrative office was directly under our top banister rail, and we had been warned that we were not to wash our hands at mealtimes from upstairs. We broke the rule constantly, just making sure that the nuns were not passing at the time we decided to wash our hands. One day I was so busy continuing an interesting conversation at lunch while washing my hands that it was a shock to discover that the dirty water had fallen on the principal nun's veil! All hell broke loose, and I was summoned downstairs. She was a dignified lady, but she was so angry at this humiliation that she made me stretch out my hand and I got two whacks with a cane. I have to admit I deserved it!

A Tiffin Carrier Lunch: Beef Olathe

Ingredients:

2 pounds of beef, preferably cubed rump roast

1 large onion, sliced thinly

6 cloves of garlic, chopped

4 green chilies, chopped

1 finger length of ginger, peeled and chopped

2 tablespoons curry leaves

1 cup of thin-sliced coconut pieces

3 tablespoons coconut oil

Salt to taste

2 teaspoons turmeric powder

3 teaspoons chili powder

4 teaspoons coriander powder

2 teaspoons garlic powder

2 teaspoons ground black pepper

2 teaspoons onion powder

3 tablespoons apple cider vinegar

Wash the beef well and put it in a pot with 3 cups of water, salt, 1 teaspoon of turmeric powder, 1 teaspoon of chili powder, 1 teaspoon of garlic powder, 1 teaspoon of ground black pepper, 1 teaspoon of onion powder, and 3 tablespoons of apple cider vinegar. This is one instance where instead of using the pressure cooker, the texture of the beef would be better if you boiled it at medium-high for 1 hour. Stir it occasionally to make sure it is not sticking to the pot. If the water runs low, add a little bit more water to the pot. In a skillet at medium-high pour the coconut oil, add the onions, garlic, green chilies, ginger, curry leaves and the coconut pieces. Stir it until the mixture turns slightly brown and add 1 teaspoon of turmeric powder, 2 teaspoons of chili powder, 4 teaspoons of coriander powder, 1 teaspoon of garlic powder, 1 teaspoon of ground black pepper, and 1 teaspoon of onion powder, and stir for a minute. Add the beef and mix it well. Continue stirring until most of the water is gone and the beef starts to brown slightly, giving it a light, crunchy texture. It can be served with rice or as an appetizer.

18

A Tale of Two Porkers: Pork Vindaloo

Chummar Elayappan *was my mother's paternal uncle,* and he lived in a house above the steep embankment that led to my grandmother's house in Mattom. Hard rocks lined one side of the dirt road. On the other side was Chummar Elayappan's vast property. Many of the Syrian Christian names were derivatives of the names of the apostles. Chummar was native for Simon, Yaakob or Chakko was the term for Jacob, and Poulose was the derivative for Paul. Chummar Elayappan's house was a little more modern than my grandmother's in the sense that it had two toilets inside, but the bathhouse was still outside. He was a good-looking man with great features and a ruddy, robust complexion. He was also an educated man and served as the principal of the local school in his professional capacity. Fluent in English, he also liked to try out new crops in his holdings. In addition to the many paddy fields, he also had a big nest of lovebirds, a fish tank, a beehive, and several other interesting undertakings. Every year he would undergo the yearly Ayurvedic ritual massage in order to rejuvenate the body and mind. This involved filling a small canoe like trough with seasoned coconut oil (seasoned with tulsi leaves, peppercorns, and other herbs prescribed by the local Ayurvedic doctor) and the patient would lie in the oil. The masseuse would then hold himself up by strong ropes tied to the ceiling beam positioned above the trough, and with his feet, he would massage the body in rhythmic steps. This was a weeklong treatment and hence considered an expensive luxury. But old-timers swear by its efficacy as the testimony to their longevity and general good health.

When we were spending a few days with her, my grandmother, after all her cooking chores were over, would head over to the bathing room at the end of the corridor. This room had a big walled-off enclosure about four feet in height, which could be filled with water. The maid Kaali would draw pail after pail of water from the well and fill this square chamber. She would then warm up water in a big cauldron on the stove and would bring a bucket of that hot water into the bathroom for my grandmother to bathe. There were no showers and you had to use a plastic dipper to scoop the water and mix it in the bucket at the right temperature for a bath. My mother would scramble to put us in our Sunday best because my grandmother was very particular. After her bath, my grandmother would put on a good sari and what she called "snow" (Pond's Cream) on her face. Next came a layer of Cuticurra powder that she would liberally apply to our faces as well. Then she would go to her safe and bring out a bottle of perfume (she would always have perfume because everybody knew that she loved it and so it was a common present for her), which she would gently apply to herself in a few places and then proceed to do the same for the older children like my sister and myself. Then it was off to Chummar Elayappan's house with my grandmother leading the way, holding a flashlight and all of us in tow. Chummar Elayappan's wife Mariyamkutty Elayamma was a beautiful woman who looked like an Italian Renaissance painting. With her big, soulful eyes, hooked nose, Cupid-shaped lips, plump figure, and beautiful olive complexion, she could have even passed for a Botticelli painting. She was a kind lady and would offer us some refreshments, usually jack fruit chips, banana chips, or sometimes an exotic fruit such as pomegranates or persimmons growing in their garden. Our grandmother would give us "the look" if we ever showed any over eagerness in sampling any of the snacks, because, after all, we were supposed to be young ladies with good etiquette and manners. We loved looking at their lovebirds, the talking parrots, and the cows and goats in the barn.

That particular Easter, Chummar Elayappan's pride and joy were his two white pigs. He had bought them as little piglets and had built a separate pigsty for them. He fed them the choicest grains and they were affectionately called "Sheema Pork"(White Pigs) in order to distinguish them from the darker, native variety. He was fattening them up for a wedding, and we kids got a lot of pleasure watching them wallow in the mud and slovenly walk around in their cage. They were a solid three hundred pounds each and the county had never seen pigs that big! One day in my grandmother's house, we were all sitting around and talking after breakfast when Chummar Elayappan's field hand came running. He was all out of breath, having run the two miles or so over the rocks to our house and all he could pant was, "Ayyo, pork odippoyi! Porkine kando?" ("Oh no, the porkers have run off! Did you see the pork?") Obviously someone had raised the Amber Alert after seeing the cage door open, when he went to feed the pigs and the two behemoths were nowhere in sight. Whoever was responsible was going to get a real talking to. We had not seen the pigs, and later on we heard another search party trying to locate the runaway porkers. The story had a sad ending because those pigs were a foreign breed and unused to the blazing heat of the tropics. Everyone knew that they would not be able to survive if they went out into the heat of the fields. That was the reason for the search party's desperation to find them. And, alas! After taking off, the porkers got overheated and ran into a pool of water thereby congealing the melted fat on them and essentially suffocating themselves to death. It was the news bulletin of the day.

A Tale of Two Porkers— Pork Vindaloo

Ingredients:

2 pounds of pork shoulder, preferably with a little fat, cubed

1 big onion, chopped

10 garlic cloves, chopped

4 green chilies, chopped

1 finger length of ginger, peeled and chopped

2 tablespoons coriander leaves, chopped

2 tablespoons curry leaves

Salt to taste

2 teaspoons garlic powder

2 teaspoons ground black pepper

2 teaspoons onion powder

2 teaspoons turmeric powder

3 teaspoons chili powder

4 teaspoons coriander powder

2 teaspoons garam masala

½ teaspoon methi (fenugreek) powder

4 star anise flowers

2 teaspoons black cumin seeds

6 cardamom pods

2 sticks of cinnamon

6 cloves

1 six-ounce can of tomato paste

6 tablespoons apple cider vinegar

3 tablespoons coconut oil

1 cup of water

Wash the pork well and place it in a pressure cooker along with salt, 1 teaspoon turmeric powder, 1 teaspoon chili powder, 1 teaspoon garlic powder, 1 teaspoon ground black pepper, 1 teaspoon onion powder, and 3 tablespoons of apple cider vinegar. Mix it well, put the lid on the pressure cooker, and place it on the stove at medium-high. When the pressure starts to escape from the top, put the weight on, turn the heat to medium, and cook it for 10 minutes. The pork will be tender. In a coffee grinder, grind into fine powder the cumin, star anise, cardamom, cinnamon and cloves. Pour the coconut oil into a saucepan and add to it the onions, garlic, green chilies, ginger, coriander leaves, and curry leaves. Sauté them until they are light brown, then add the salt, 1 teaspoon of turmeric powder, 2 teaspoons of chili powder, 4 teaspoons of coriander powder, 2 teaspoons of garam masala, methi powder, and the coffee grinder blend of spices. Stir well and in a minute add the can of tomato paste, 3 tablespoons of apple cider vinegar, and 1 cup of water. Empty the pork from the pressure cooker into this mixture and give it a good stir. Cover it with the lid and at medium heat cook it for about five minutes or until it reaches a steady boil. It is best served with rice or naan, roti, or any of the Indian breads.

The vindaloo, like many a pork dish, had its origins in the Portuguese colony of Goa, which is a seaside town in India. This is the reason the vindaloo has a lot of resemblance to the Portuguese and Spanish stews and most probably the introduction of tomato into the Indian diet can be traced back to these New World invaders.

19
Hostel Dinner: Saambaar and Green Beans

In college there were two kinds of students. There were the day scholars, the students who came from their homes every day to study, and there were students like me who came from some distance and stayed in the hostel provided for us. We went home only for a couple of weekends and mostly for Christmas and the end-of-the-year vacations. During our first year at the hostel, we were allotted rooms of two people each and sometimes even slightly bigger rooms of five. Six-thirty in the morning was the time for mass for all Catholic students at the hostel and the nun had even allotted specific places for us in the chapel so that at one glance she could see which students were missing mass on any particular day. In the evening we had study hours in the hall after which there would be a rosary for the Catholic girls while the non-Catholics could pursue their studies. The nun in charge of us was called "The Warden." She would regularly sneak up to the study hall gathering up her rosary beads (the stealth attack, so that the beads did not clack, clack against her habit and announce her arrival), and anyone who was found not studying and engaging in frivolous activities such as talking and laughing were invited into her room to get a stern lecture. Then it was off to dinner downstairs in the big mess hall with rows and rows of faucets and drains to wash our hands. The dining hall was arranged into tables of six and we usually sat with our friends. Like all teenagers, badmouthing authority figures and rules was our common pastime.

The nighttime meal was a simple vegetarian affair consisting usually of rice, some type of daal (lentils), and a vegetable. Imagine the racket when two hundred girls got together under one roof for dinner every night! The most common lentil preparation in the south of India is saambaar. Pungent with tamarind and tomatoes, the original saambaar is a mix of six vegetables: onions, green beans, carrots, winter melon, pumpkin, and the stringy vegetable called muringakkai (drumsticks). But in reality, it usually ends up being a mix of about three vegetables. Vegetables like green beans, spinach, melons, tapioca, and yams were all available in plenty because they grew in abundance and hence were very reasonably priced.

My friend Annie George, who was the captain of the college cricket team, and I were both students of English literature. The Poets Artists Day is a yearly celebration conducted by the literature department in order to enlighten students about the various artists and literary figures of yesteryears. The degree in literature is usually three years and the masters course is another two years. They divided us according to our degree year, and I do not remember which year it was. It may have been our very first year in literature and I believe our subject was Shakespeare. One of our friends had a cousin who built us a magnificent miniature Shakespearean theater all out of just plain matchsticks! Most of the budget (which was extremely minimal to start with) went into the making of this, and maybe it was my first lesson about not putting all your eggs in one basket! There were a few other artifacts made by the students and yet they were nowhere enough to fill the two classrooms that were allotted to us. The seniors were doing a lot of exhibits, and we were desperate not to look like total fools. We needed to make the space look beautiful and inviting because there was a prize involved. So we came up with the most scatterbrained idea.

Annie and I were in a hurry to finish our dinner because we had places to go. Sister Alonzo was the chief of botany, and she had a beautiful botanical garden with various specimens of plants in pots. It was her pride and joy, and she would take her students on a tour of these where they would study the various flora and fauna. The garden was situated at the front entrance of the main college near the main gates. Our hostel was situated a little distance away from the main college. So Annie and I snuck out after dinner and made our way behind the bushes to the botanical garden. As we were calculating which pots were light enough to carry off, to our dismay, we saw the security guard (he was called a gurkha because he was a retired foot soldier from the famous northern Gurkha regiment in the Indian Army which had a reputation for being fierce fighters) coming on his nightly inspection with his two Alsatian canine friends. We crouched behind the flowerpots, terrified that the dogs would give us away. And sure enough, the two of them began barking in our direction and straining at their leash. It was terrifying and exhilarating at the same time! "Arf, Arf!" went the guardians of our college. The guard looked irritated and yanked at their leash exclaiming, "Badmash, Kuthe, Chalo!" ("Stupid dogs, let's go!") Pheeew! He was so sure that they were after a squirrel or a rabbit. Little did he know that there were two stupid girls hiding behind one of the flowerpots. We must have giggled for hours afterwards.

The next day at the exhibition who should come along to view the exhibits but sister Alonzo herself! She looked around and exclaimed, "I have some of these specimens in my botanical garden!" We had our answer ready and informed her how they came from the garden of one of our friends whose father was a very big industrialist in town known for his family's magnificent garden. She was a sweet nun and seemed satisfied enough with our fib. That night the adventure began all over again when we had to return the pots. This time we were seasoned criminals and when the dogs barked, we informed the guard that we were entrusted to return the pots used for the function by sister Alonzo herself. I don't believe we won anything for that Poets Artists Day!

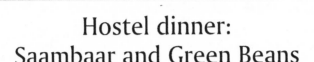

Hostel dinner: Saambaar and Green Beans

Saambaar

Ingredients:

1 cup of toor daal (yellow lentil), washed and drained

⅓ cup masoor daal (orange lentil), washed and drained

Salt to taste

Half an onion, chopped

2 green chilies, chopped

1 finger length ginger, peeled and chopped

4 tablespoons curry leaves

1 bell pepper, chopped

4 tablespoons cilantro leaves, chopped

1 six-oz can of crushed tomatoes

1 teaspoon of tamarind paste

1 tablespoon asafetida

1 teaspoon methi (fenugreek) powder

1 teaspoon garlic powder

3 tablespoons saambaar masala packet powder

6 tablespoons coconut oil

2 tablespoons black mustard seeds

6 pods of dry chilies

8 cups of water

Place the toor daal and the masoor daal in a pressure cooker along with salt and 2 cups of water. Put the lid on and set the heat to medium-high. When the steam starts to appear at the top, place the weight and cook it at medium for 10 minutes. Into this daal mixture, add the chopped onion, green chilies, ginger, cilantro leaves, chopped bell pepper, the crushed tomatoes, the tamarind paste, and the 6 cups of water. Pour the coconut oil into a small skillet over medium-high heat and, when hot, add the mustard seeds, dried chili pods, and the curry leaves to it. When the mustard seeds start popping, add the asafetida, methi (fenugreek) powder, garlic powder, and the saambaar masala powder. Pour this into the lentil mixture and cook it at medium stirring constantly for about 10 minutes or until it bubbles.

Green Beans

Ingredients:

1 pound of green beans, washed and chopped into 2-inch-long pieces

Salt to taste

Half an onion, chopped

2 green chilies, chopped

4 cloves of garlic, chopped

1 inch of ginger, peeled and chopped

2 tablespoons curry leaves

3 tablespoons coconut oil

2 teaspoons garlic powder

2 teaspoons ground black pepper

2 teaspoons dried chopped chives

2 teaspoons chopped parsley

1 packet of unsweetened grated fresh coconut (frozen)

1 tablespoon soy sauce

¼ cup of water

In a skillet at medium-high, pour the coconut oil and add the onions, green chilies, ginger, garlic, curry leaves and the fresh coconut. When the coconut starts to brown slightly, add the garlic powder, ground black pepper, chives, parsley and stir it for a minute. To this add the soy sauce, ¼ cup water, and the chopped beans, and give it a good stir. Put the lid on and cook it at medium for 5 minutes. It will be a delicious accompaniment to any dinner.

20

Mango Cheesecake

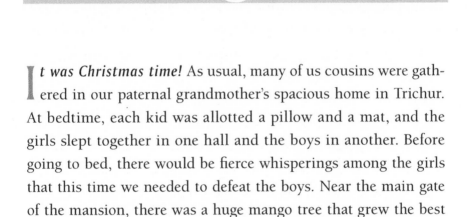

I t was Christmas time! As usual, many of us cousins were gathered in our paternal grandmother's spacious home in Trichur. At bedtime, each kid was allotted a pillow and a mat, and the girls slept together in one hall and the boys in another. Before going to bed, there would be fierce whisperings among the girls that this time we needed to defeat the boys. Near the main gate of the mansion, there was a huge mango tree that grew the best Chandrakaran mangoes (a specific variety), colloquially known as "chappikudian maanga." These mangoes are usually smaller and very sweet. They do not have much of a pulp that can be cut with a knife. This mango is best eaten when ripe by first squishing it in your hand and then making a small opening at the top of it and sucking out the delicious watery pulp like you would with a straw. Trichur in December had some fierce winds coming in through the Western Ghat Mountains called "vrishchikakkaatte." So during the night, the winds would have swayed the mango tree with all their might and in the morning, the grounds around it were littered with beautiful ripe little mangoes. The discussion of the girls was all about getting up even earlier than the boys so that the girl's team could collect most of the mangoes, leaving the boys with very few. We derived quite a bit of pleasure in waiting till the boys got up before starting to eat the little mangoes right in front of them!

My grandparents had made sure that the compound had many exclusive varieties of mango trees like Pryor, Mulgove, and Salem. They had also planted Sapota, custard apple, and guava trees. The mango trees had the best branches and hence we would climb them, pluck the green unripe mangoes, cut them into pieces, season them with salt, chili powder, onions, and a little coconut oil, and eat them. My grandmother did not approve of us plucking the mangoes before they were ripe so she forbade us from doing it. But the old lady had not accounted for her very crafty grandkids. Some smartass pointed out that she only said we couldn't pluck the unripe mango from the tree, so we were free to climb the tree and eat the mango while it was still hanging on the tree! So it was not uncommon to see mango seeds hanging on a tree!

When we started our small restaurant, "India Café" sixteen years ago, we wanted even the desserts to be mostly Indian. We tried to make gulab jamuns, rasmalai, and other such Indian sweets, but found out, just as I had found out earlier from our home parties, that Americans in general find Indian desserts cloyingly sweet. Hence we came up with an Indian-themed American dessert. We were the first to make it, and we are proud to say that even now it is still a good seller.

Mango Cheesecake

Ingredients:

Four packets of Philadelphia soft cream cheese kept at room temperature for an hour

½ cup Alphonso mango pulp

1 cup sugar

4 eggs

2 tablespoons vanilla extract

1 tablespoon all-purpose flour

1 tablespoon sour cream

3 sleeves of Oreo cookies

Half a stick of butter

In a food processor, place the Oreo cookies, close the lid and powder them. Warm the butter in a small bowl for about 30 seconds in the microwave. Next, in a cheesecake pan that has been thoroughly sprayed with Pam, pour the contents of the food processor, add the butter, and mix together with your hand. Spread it evenly at the bottom of the pan. It is good if the crumbs extend a little bit up the side of the pan. Cover the bottom of the pan with aluminum foil and place it on a cookie sheet. In a preheated 350° oven, bake it for 10 minutes, then take it out and let it cool. Spray the mixing bowl of a cake Mixer with Pam. Pour in the sugar and eggs and start beating at low speed with the balloon whisk, adding little dollops of cream cheese till you exhaust all four packets. Increase the speed about two notches and add the vanilla, mango pulp, and sour cream and keep on beating. Increase the speed to the maximum for one minute and then bring down the speed to medium and add your flour. Keep working the machine for another two minutes until the mixture is smooth and creamy. Do not overwork the mixture. Pour the cheese mixture on top of the Oreo cookie crust and bake in a 350° oven for 45 minutes. Gently pull out the rack and examine the cake. If it has not started slightly browning at the top, put it back in for another 20 minutes at which time take it out and let it cool. I usually find that it is easier to cut the cheesecake after it has been frozen overnight.

21

Kerala Christmas Cake

Christmas was a very special time for Indian Catholics. There were no wild shopping sprees or extravagant presents exchanged. We might get one special dress each, stitched by the tailor who came home to take measurements. Most of Christmas was spent in celebrations at church for several days. Elaborate mangers would be put up at homes and churches, and many local youth would organize carol singing groups. Sometimes these groups were organized by young boys because they had a need for some special sports equipment like a football or cricket bats or hockey sticks. They would come between 9 and 12 o'clock with a skinny, ragtag Santa in tow, whose only job seemed to be bouncing his head like one of the Indian dancing dolls! Their music was equally uninspiring, and when everyone would give them a few bucks, they were thrilled.

Christmas morning was usually spent in my maternal grandmother's three-hundred-year-old home in Mattom. My grandmother would wake up very early in the morning and start the preparations for the afternoon feast. Her help, Kaali, would have come down from her little hut up in the hills, traipsing through the thick undergrowth, barefooted. She would go straight to the henhouse, and after much discussion with my grandmother as to which chicken was the most plump, she would catch it and very nonchalantly wring its neck! The hen would flop around for a minute or two and then it was time to dip it in hot water in order to pluck the feathers. Then the chicken would be quickly passed through a shallow fire of dried coconut fronds. This is to burn away all the fine down feathers. Then it was onto the chopping block and the process of roasting the chicken on the fire in a wide vessel called a "urili," usually made with an alloy of brass and copper.

While all these activities are going on in the background, we would be getting ready to go to church for the 9 o'clock mass. My grandmother would have reminded my mother to bring all of our finest dresses as well as some heavy gold jewelry. Thus dressed like Christmas trees with heavy gold jewelry that was way too grown-up for us, we would line up for my grandmother's inspection. She would run a practiced eye over us and might suggest a modification here or there, usually in the "more" direction than the "less." She would then bring out her infamous "snow" (Pond's Cream) and, in the words of my brother, make us look like ghosts! This glitterati procession marched to church and was always late. But instead of taking up the back rows, my grandmother marched us to the front of the church, making sure the whole congregation had a good look at her overly dressed grandchildren. The vicar, who was usually the beneficiary of her generous cooking skills, would look at us with benevolence. After the mass and introductions all around, we would traipse back to the house and the sumptuous roast dinner that was awaiting us. By this time we kids would have started to get impatient because we were waiting for the arrival of our father. He would come in with his usual loud good cheer and compliment his mother-in-law profusely for her cooking prowess.

After lunch, our family would make our farewells and my grandmother would give each of us kids pocket money, with me, the oldest getting the most and then going in descending order to the youngest. We would pile into the car and go to Koratty, where the company that my father worked for was situated. The company Christmas celebrations were about to begin. It was all very exciting! We would change from our traditional outfits of skirt and blouse to more modern outfits like dresses and even hot pants when they were the style in the United States (my mother had brought them back when she went with Dad for his training in Montreal). My grandmother never approved of us wearing jeans, but we wore them anyway, in the compound. We would all gather at the clubhouse, eagerly awaiting the arrival of Santa. It was a most unique tradition. Santa (usually the managers took turns at becoming Santa and the older kids would try to guess who it was) would come on top of an elephant with the mahout (the elephant trainer) and there would be traditional Kerala-style shirtless drummers accompanying the elephant. There would be someone playing the "naadaswaram" (wind instrument) and the traditional cymbals. It was a perfect blending of Eastern and Western cultures and something that will stay in my memory forever. Words come up short trying to describe the exhilaration of watching Santa make his grand entrance from the tall company gates, the elephant with its stately gait, the loud drums and accompaniments! It was indeed any child's dream Christmas. The presents passed down from Santa were usually practical gifts hurriedly wrapped by our parents and sent to the clubhouse. After tea would come the elephant rides. Anyone who wanted to could get a ride on the elephant around the club lawn. We lived for that. It was a perfect Christmas.

Christmas cake is a tradition that is followed in many variations all over Kerala. Housewives would start their jars of currants (raisins) soaked in brandy a month before Christmas. This is why I call it the drunken raisin cake! Closer to Christmas, the ovens—whether it be my mother's "Baby Belling" imported from England or the rustic countertop plug-in variety used in a lot of Kerala homes in those days—were working overtime chugging out Kerala Christmas cakes which were offered routinely to any guest who came calling.

Kerala Christmas Cake

Ingredients:

2 cups of raisins (golden or black) immersed fully in rum for one week. (I find that the caramelization of the rum adds a greater flavor than brandy.)

2 packets of Duncan Hines yellow butter cake flour

1 stick of butter

1 ½ cups sugar

¼ cup vegetable oil

4 eggs

2 tablespoons vanilla extract

1 tablespoon pumpkin spice mix

1 tablespoon sour cream

1 tablespoon all-purpose flour

¼ cup water

¼ cup rum (Captain Morgan's spiced rum preferred)

1 cup cashew nuts, chopped but not powdered

Preheat the oven to 350 degrees. In a saucepan sprayed with Pam, pour in half a cup of sugar and place it over medium-high heat. Stir it constantly, and when the sugar starts browning just at the point when it is about to burn (do not let it burn or it will taste nasty), pour in ¼ cup water, the rum, and the vanilla, and turn off the heat. Keep stirring so that the melted sugar dissolves and, if need be, strain it into another bowl to get rid of sugar particles. Take out your cake Mixer with the balloon whisk attachment. Spray the mixer bowl with Pam. Put your eggs in it along with

1 cup of sugar and the pumpkin spice, and start the whisk going at medium speed. Then add your melted butter, vegetable oil, and sour cream as well as the caramelized liquid we had made earlier. Increase the speed by one notch and add the contents of the cake packets a little at a time so as to prevent clumping. Scrape the sides of the bowl if necessary, add the 1 tablespoon of all-purpose flour and continue mixing.

Increase the speed to maximum for about 2 minutes and then reduce it all the way to low. At this time, add your raisins and the chopped cashew nuts and continue mixing for about 2 minutes more. Spray Pam liberally on two 8-inch round cake tins and coat them with flour. Shake it around and dump the excess flour from the cake pans. Spoon the batter into the two cake pans, making sure that both the pans get an equal amount of all the ingredients. In a preheated 350° oven, bake the cakes on the center rack for 45 minutes and then observe. The top might start to burn, and it would not have been cooked through. Loosely cover the tops with aluminum foil and continue baking for about 20 minutes more. Take it out and let it rest for 3 hours at which time it can be taken out of the baking dish and presented on a platter. Not only does it make a great dessert, but they make very good gifts at Christmas time.

22

An Unexpected Visitor: Kashmiri Chicken

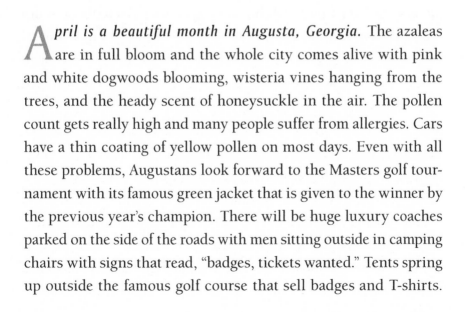

April is a beautiful month in Augusta, Georgia. The azaleas are in full bloom and the whole city comes alive with pink and white dogwoods blooming, wisteria vines hanging from the trees, and the heady scent of honeysuckle in the air. The pollen count gets really high and many people suffer from allergies. Cars have a thin coating of yellow pollen on most days. Even with all these problems, Augustans look forward to the Masters golf tournament with its famous green jacket that is given to the winner by the previous year's champion. There will be huge luxury coaches parked on the side of the roads with men sitting outside in camping chairs with signs that read, "badges, tickets wanted." Tents spring up outside the famous golf course that sell badges and T-shirts.

Because of the throng of international tourists who descend on Augusta at this time, many of the native residents choose to rent their homes to companies and go on vacation. The money is good and it is tax free. The traffic gridlocks can also be a problem when one is trying to go to work downtown. With all this, it is still a very exciting time for the city and the state and you can see dozens of corporate and private jets parked in neat rows at both Daniel Field Airport as well as Augusta Regional Airport. Presidents fly in for the occasion, as do heads of corporations who make Atlanta their home base and fly in on their private jets each day. With all the rich and the famous coming to town, it is one of the biggest boosts for the economy of our city as well as the state.

In general, our small café does not benefit greatly from this tournament. The tourists often confine themselves to areas they can walk to and hence many of the restaurants in and around the Masters Golf Course do brisk business at that time. The schools are usually out and our regular clientele would have rented their homes and gone to one of the many beaches in Georgia or South Carolina. Other than the occasional Brit who comes in search of Indian food, it is generally a slow time for us. It is on one such Tuesday that a group of people came into India Café. They ordered their beers and studied the menu carefully. There was a very tall man who looked Indian who seemed to know his way around the menu. He was the one who was recommending dishes to the others and when my husband went to take their orders, he was the one who ordered. It was a very balanced array of dishes—chicken and lamb with an assortment of rice and naan. I started to work on their order and when dinner was served, they seemed overall pleased with it. You could hear them talking about golf and we assumed that they were also part of the wide world of golf enthusiasts who had come to watch their favorite game. When the time came to pay, the tall man extended his card to my husband and told him to put it on his tab. That is when my husband suddenly noticed that the name on the card read "Vijay Singh" and it was a golf card. He couldn't believe that he had just served dinner to one of golf's greatest players and Masters champion Mr. Vijay Singh! So he had to go back to the table and ask him, "Are you *the* Mr. Vijay Singh?" The champion laughed and said simply, "Yes, I am." My husband and I had a high-level corporate meeting in the kitchen. In hushed whispers we were trying to figure out the best course of action. As our honored customer, is it proper for us to intrude on his privacy by asking him for a photograph or an autograph? We had never had a celebrity of this magnitude before and we were at a loss.

My husband and I decided that the best course of action was not to bother him with it and so we came outside to tell him how honored we were that he chose to dine with us. We could only hope that when we related the story to our friends later on, they would not think that it was just a figment of our imagination! When the group saw us coming to their table in the dining room, the man sitting next to Mr. Singh, who seemed like a South African, jumped up and asked us, "Don't you want any pictures with Vijay?" Did we ever! Mr. Singh was a most gracious gentleman and he posed with us for pictures, even helping us when we did not know quite how to use our new Apple phone! We were so thrilled. The photo still hangs in the café and many customers still enjoy looking at it, as we do. The only problem is that Mr. Vijay Singh is about 6'7" tall, and at barely 5'2", I look like I am just 4 feet tall! He came the next year too, and they celebrated how he had made the cut. I noticed that they ordered the Kashmiri chicken this time as well. So in my mind, Kashmiri chicken has a very special place.

Kashmiri Chicken

Ingredients:

10 chicken thighs or breasts or a combination of both, skinned and washed, cut into medium pieces

1 large onion, chopped

6 cloves of garlic, chopped

2 green chilies, chopped

1 finger length of ginger, chopped

2 tablespoons cilantro leaves, chopped

Salt to taste

2 teaspoons turmeric

2 teaspoons chili powder

2 teaspoons garam masala

Half teaspoon of methi (fenugreek) powder

2 teaspoons garlic powder

2 teaspoons ground black pepper

2 teaspoons onion powder

2 tablespoons tandoori masala powder

One 6-oz. can crushed tomatoes

Half a cup of sour cream

1 tablespoon of black raisins

¼ cup of cashews

3 tablespoons apple cider vinegar

1 stick of butter

3 tablespoons vegetable oil

1 cup of water

Put the raisins and the cashews with a little water into a blender and blend well. Place the chicken, salt, 1 teaspoon garlic powder, 1 teaspoon ground black pepper, 1 teaspoon onion powder, 1 teaspoon

turmeric powder, 1 teaspoon chili powder, and 3 tablespoons of apple cider vinegar into a pressure cooker. Close the lid and put it on high heat. When the steam starts to come from the top, put the weight on and cook for 12 minutes at medium temperature. This will make the chicken tender.

In a deep saucepan at medium heat, pour in the vegetable oil and the stick of butter. Add the onions, garlic, green chilies, ginger and the cilantro leaves and stir it around. When the mixture turns slightly brown, add salt, 1 teaspoon turmeric powder, 1 teaspoon chili powder, 1 teaspoon garlic powder, 1 teaspoon ground black pepper, 1 teaspoon onion powder, garam masala, methi or fenugreek powder, and the tandoori masala powder. Stir it for 2 minutes and add the crushed tomatoes and the sour cream as well as the water. Add the purée of raisins and cashews and mix it well. Add the chicken from the pressure cooker and mix everything thoroughly. Cover with a lid and cook it for about 5 minutes until the liquid starts bubbling.

This is a Mughlai preparation and hence eaten best with rice or naan.

23

Consolation Prize: Masala Dosa and Puri Potato

addy was the one who first introduced me to tennis at the age of six. The wooden racket was far too big, but I felt privileged that my father was teaching me such a grown-up game. I had watched my father and his colleagues play and it looked like a lot of fun! Daddy was way ahead of his time in the sense that he did not see much distinction between a daughter and a son. If you were good at something, he was only too glad to cheer you on. My earliest and only tennis coach was Chidambaram. He was the coach for the Kerala team and worked from Trivandrum (the state of Kerala's capital city), but in the summers, he was hired by the company to coach the managers' kids in the compound. Sometimes when the schedule was made for coaching times, your turn might be at 6:30 in the morning. It was difficult to get up, but once you ran up the street to the club and the courts, Chidambaram Uncle, as we used to call him, kept us hopping with his raspy voice. "Don't dance, Priya," he would yell out, correcting the two-step forehand that was so characteristic of me. If a particular shot of yours was not the way he wanted it, the punishment was to run round the courts ten times.

Our evenings followed the same pattern. We came back from school at about 5 o'clock, quickly wolfed down the snacks that mummy would have made, and hurriedly putting on our Keds (believe it or not it was the thin Keds and not tennis shoes like now). We would take our rackets (we used to spell it "racquets") out of their brackets and race to the tennis courts for a couple of sets. By then the adults would have started coming to play and would shoo us off the courts. Then we would proceed to the mill area a mile away, play shuttlecock in the covered courts, and by nightfall come back home side again. If it was summertime, we might stop for a game or two of table tennis in the clubhouse and then beg Mom to let us jump in the pool. Even after she had given permission to go to the pool, she would go upstairs to the balcony and survey the pool area. If there was any person of male gender between the ages of seven and seventy, permission would be withdrawn! I never understood the point of getting swimsuits (or swimming trunks as they were called then) from England and then not being allowed to go when there were people around to admire them!

I had become fairly good at tennis in a large part because my father took a great deal of interest in improving my game. He himself was a very good player, and even in his 70s when he visited us in the states, people were amazed at how good he still was. When it came to mixed doubles, my mother did not want me to play with

118

anybody other than my father as my partner. My father and I, along with many of our club players, used to compete at a club called The Banerjee Club in Trichur, which was my father's hometown. Our players did reasonably well as did some of the members of Banerjee Club. One year I had the thrill of becoming the Kerala State Women's Champion of the Year. However, the next year, the governing committee of Banerjee Club decided that they needed to bring more competition in the female division. That was the year they invited Amrita Ahluwalia, India's number-four player at the time. In the company compound where we lived, when we played tennis, we played in skirts or dresses, but mom decided that if I was to play in Trichur to a larger audience of the general public, I should be more modestly attired so as not to compromise my marriage eligibility later on. So she had me wearing blue stirrup pants with a white top, the general idea being that I should look good and modest even if I played lousy!

On the day of the tournament, Dad and Mom would come to my college hostel after my classes and pick me up. Mom would have some snack for me to munch on while we went to Banerjee Club. When we arrived at the club there was a lot of excitement because one of India's best players was going to play. Most of Trichur had come out to watch the match, and they sat in the stands, almost all of them wearing their dhotis. Amrita Ahluwalia came out just before the coin toss, gave me a scornful look, and said, "Are you going to be playing in *that*?" My heart sank, and my confidence plunged even lower. I had never played a match in which I was so much out of my depth. I was losing badly, and when the rest time came, I hear a familiar voice in the crowd shouting my name. When I looked up, it is none other than my very own dear uncle (my father's younger brother, Johnny Uncle, as we called him) who had

119

imbibed a little too much from his brandy bottle and was waving a newspaper cone of peanuts at me saying, "Priye idu thinna mathi, ellam shariyavum!" ("You just have to eat this, everything will be fine!") I have never before or after wanted to disown a member of my family as much as I wanted to disown him at that time!

The line umpire was Johnny Uncle's buddy whom he called, "Jangedy Jaan,"—a shriveled up old guy who was also his drinking partner. This joker thought that he would help me out. And when one of Ms. Ahluwalia's shots grazed the sideline, he called out, "Out . . . Way out!" and the whole Trichur crowd roared in appreciation because I was, after all, their hometown girl! Even up until ten years ago, when I used to go to the fish market in Trichur, there would be vendors from the various fish stalls calling out, "Priye, ithu nalla meanaa!" ("Priya, this is good fish!") and my mother would chuckle and say, "Your Banerjee fans are calling you!" Needless to say, I had a very humiliating defeat at the hands of Amrita Ahluwalia.

After the tournament we headed to our usual place to eat— Pathan's Café, which was a vegetarian restaurant with good snacks and great coffee. In those days when you went out eating it was either to a Biriyani joint, a vegetarian place, or if you wanted something more fancy, a Chinese restaurant. Daddy was a popular customer at Pathan's, and we would always be assigned the best waiter. They were always thrilled when Dad in his usual fashion would order two of everything—masala dosas, my mother's favorite puri potatoes, dahi (yogurt) vadas, saambaar vadas, and six coffees. This was all for three people! Masala dosa is our variation of the French crepe', but made with white lentils. Puri is a fried round thin bread and eaten with potatoes. Masala dosa is usually served with potato masala inside the dosa and is dipped in coconut chutney and saambaar (the recipe for which is given in chapter 20).

Masala Dosa

Ingredients:

1 cup of urad daal, washed

1 cup of long grain rice, washed

2 cups rice flour

3 cups water

1 teaspoon salt

¼ cup coconut oil

We use a stone grinder at the café, but at home it is more practical to blend the washed rice and urad daal in a blender with 3 cups of water. Grind it until it is smooth and add the rice flour and salt and mix it well with a whisk until the mixture is smooth and has the consistency of pancake batter. If it is too thick, add more water and whisk. Cover the batter with aluminum foil and keep it aside for about 6 to 8 hours in a warm place. The batter will have fermented and little bubbles can be seen. Place a nonstick pan sprayed with Pam over the fire at medium heat, spoon in the batter, and spread it in a circular motion until it becomes a thin layer. Spread 1 teaspoon of coconut oil on top of the dosa in the pan. When the bottom starts to brown, take it out with a thin spatula and serve it with chutney and saambaar. It can be made thinner or thicker depending on how you spread it.

Potato Masala for Dosa or Puri
Ingredients:

Four large baking potatoes, peeled, cubed, and washed

1 cup frozen peas

One large onion, chopped

Two green chilies, chopped

1 finger length of ginger, peeled and chopped

Salt to taste

1 teaspoon turmeric powder

1 teaspoon chili powder

Half a teaspoon of methi (fenugreek) powder

1 teaspoon garlic powder

1 teaspoon ground black pepper

2 teaspoons chopped dried chives

2 teaspoons chopped dried parsley

¼ cup of coconut oil

2 tablespoons black mustard seeds

Six pods dried chilies

2 tablespoons chopped cilantro

2 tablespoons curry leaves

In a pot, place the potatoes, salt, and water and cook for about 15 minutes or until tender. Drain out water and mash the potatoes with a potato masher. Pour the coconut oil into a saucepan on medium-high heat. When hot, add the mustard seeds, dried chili pods, and curry leaves. Once the mustard starts popping, add the onion, green chilies, ginger and cilantro leaves. To this also add the frozen peas and keep stirring. When the mixture turns translucent, add turmeric powder, chili powder, fenugreek powder, garlic powder, ground black pepper, chives, and parsley. Stir for a couple more minutes and pour in the mashed potatoes. Mix thoroughly and cook for about 5 minutes at very low heat with the pan covered and mixing often. This is your potato masala. This can also be eaten with puris.

Coconut Chutney
Ingredients:

1 packet frozen unsweetened grated coconut

Half an onion, quartered

2 green chilies

1 finger length ginger, peeled

2 teaspoons tamarind pulp

Salt to taste

1 teaspoon chili powder

1 teaspoon garlic powder

1 teaspoon ground black pepper

1 teaspoon methi (fenugreek) powder

3 tablespoons coconut oil

2 tablespoons black mustard seeds

6 dried chili pods

2 tablespoons curry leaves

2 cups of water

In a blender, place the coconut, onion, green chilies, ginger, salt, chili powder, garlic powder, ground black pepper, and tamarind pulp. Pour in the 2 cups of water and grind it into a smooth mixture. Pour the coconut oil into a small skillet at medium-high heat and put in the mustard seeds, dry chili pods, and curry leaves. When the mustard starts popping, add the methi (fenugreek) powder, and pour the seasoned oil into the chutney. Stir well and serve with dosa.

Puri (Fried Bread)

Ingredients:

1 cup of atta (fine wheat flour available in Indian grocery stores)

½ a teaspoon of salt

3 tablespoons yogurt

2 tablespoons vegetable oil

Water as needed

3 cups of vegetable oil for frying

In a mixing bowl, place the flour, salt, yogurt, and oil and mix it thoroughly. Add half a cup of water at first to the dough, and keep on adding more water as needed to make a soft dough, and knead it until soft, like you would for bread. Cover it and let rest for 10 minutes. You can make the dough in your Kitchen Aid cake mixer as well using a dough hook. With your hands, make small balls (the size of a small lime) of dough. Spread a newspaper or some paper towels on a cookie sheet. Using a rolling pin (you can also use a manual or electric tortilla maker) roll it into four-inch wide, thin rounds and place them carefully on the cookie sheet. In a wok, heat the vegetable oil to medium and when the oil reaches a temperature of about 350°, slide in the puris one at a time, cooking both sides until it puffs up and is light brown in color. Place on a platter lined with paper towels to drain out any excess oil. Serve with the potato masala described above. Puri and potato can be a breakfast dish or a delicious snack.

Maternal Grandmother (Grandma Thresia)

Paternal Grandfather (Rao Sahib Raphael Parambi)

Maternal aunt

Paternal aunts

Parents

Parents' wedding day

My mother and her friends doing the "Thiruvaathirakkali"
(the traditional Onam dance)

Author and Mother

Maternal Grandparents with Author

Growing up in India

The author and siblings with friend Rohini

Family vacation at the Beach

The Author with sister Deepa

Jamuna School

Author in a school performance

24

The Russian Circus:
Maharani Peanuts

Daddy's hometown of Trichur was in many ways a small enclave of culture and the arts. The town's businessmen had always patronized the various arts institutions, and it was a point of pride that they had a cultural center like Kalaanilayam situated in the heart of town. Many artists, both in drama and cinema, had their first breaks in this venerable institution, and some of them even kept the name of the institution before their own given names. My father had a big interest in all things cultural; being a small-time artist himself, he has dabbled a little in acting, Kathakali (native malayali dance-drama), and other amateur theater productions. He loved the cinema and even when we had classes the next day, at dinnertime he would suddenly make the decision to go for a midnight movie! He was also a great fan of Malayalam dramas, the productions of various theater companies like the Allappey theaters or the Kalaamandalam troupe. My younger siblings who went to the company English school (it had not been established when I started school) did not much care for these productions, and hence I was the only one who went with my parents to watch them. We would buy tickets and sit in hastily constructed auditoriums which would have bare dirt floors and only a thatched roof to keep out the elements. I do not know how much my mother enjoyed these nighttime soirées, because she came from Madras and was used to more sophisticated Western entertainment. Besides, she did not learn Malayalam as a formal language in school, and hence could not follow the overly literary, flowery language used in drama in those days. There were very few female characters in dramas because of the lack of availability and all characters had kabuki-like faces painted with zinc-white (to make them look fairer) and blood-red lips (considered more attractive, I suppose). The men all had hairdos like pompadours and all the characters, whether they were acting as a cultured teacher or a simple laborer, spoke in exaggerated high literary Malayalam. The emotions portrayed were just as grand. A simple disagreement between a husband and wife looked like a battle of Shakespearean proportions. I was impressed!

Another outing I remember distinctly was when daddy took us to see the traveling Russian Circus. We were spending a weekend at my grandmother's in Trichur and the Russian Circus was in town. I can still feel the excitement of waiting near the ticket booth while my father was buying the tickets because you could smell the tigers, the lions, and the elephants! Inside the big tent the show was magnificent. The Russian acrobats were world-class, and I remember watching the high wire act and thinking that I wanted to do that some day. All those graceful ladies in leotards and glittering pantyhose with pumps on their feet going through various contortions . . . it was just beautiful. They would swing gracefully in the air and exchange swings; when they flew back to their side, they would be scooped up by such handsome, gallant, strong guys. My career goals were set.

Back at home, I was still thinking about the circus. We thought that with the four of us kids and our neighboring friend Jomon, we could pull off some of the circus stunts. We found a small plank that the workmen had discarded and raised it by placing three bricks under it. My little brother's wooden kid's highchair was placed on one end of the seesaw. At the other end, we positioned my mother's high stool that she used in the kitchen. The idea was that our friend Jomon, who was a big, tall guy, would jump from the stool onto one end of the seesaw. At the other end of the seesaw, we placed our sister Sheefa, who was very skinny. We had the law of physics down pat. Jomon jumped and Sheefa flew up in the air and landed in the highchair. Well, actually she sort of fell onto the leg rest and frantically scrambled into the highchair. We were indeed ready for the big tent! This went on a couple of times, and it looked like my sister was having too good a time. So I decided to try it for myself. It is worth mentioning that I was not built waiflike like my sister. I took my position at the other end, and on cue, Jomon jumped. I did get airborne for a minute and landed on the highchair with a big thud—and it fell apart. Jomon took off for his house, and I was left to explain to my mom why my brother's highchair was now a heap of wood on the lawn.

When we were young, at any of the events, whether cinema, drama, or sports tournaments, the predominant snack was always peanuts. They would be sold in little newspaper cones, and I do not remember anyone having an allergy to peanuts. We served peanuts in various ways for cocktails, as in-between-meals snacks, and would even grind them into chutneys.

Maharani Peanuts

Ingredients:

2 cups of unsalted peanuts with their skins off

1 onion, chopped

4 green chilies, chopped

2 tablespoons curry leaves

Salt to taste

1 teaspoon chili powder

2 tablespoons coconut oil

Place the coconut oil, peanuts, and the curry leaves into a wok at medium heat. Stir it constantly so that it does not burn. When the peanuts start browning, add the salt and chili powder and toss it around. After a minute, turn off the stove and add the onion and green chilies. It is a great cocktail snack.

25

The General's Visit: Onion Bhajias

*O*ur restaurant *India Café was opened in 2004* and it is still in operation. When my youngest child was ready to go to college, my daughter Kavya was extremely concerned. I had been a very active mother, preparing all their meals, and transporting them to soccer, ballet, piano, cross-country, tennis, Red Cross, and other academic activities like science fairs. In between all this there were numerous commitments to the various cultural organizations like the Malayali Association of Augusta as well as the greater umbrella organization, the Indian Cultural Association of Augusta. The theme of these organizations was that no child who wanted to participate was left out. They would get to participate in some way whether it was in dance, drama, or as volunteers for various cultural and charitable events. It was a busy life, and the children got to know each other really well while participating in the many programs. So when my second and youngest child was ready for college my daughter was worried that I would be at a loss for things to do. In fact she was the one who came with me when we were scouting for possible venues to open our restaurant. Being a first-generation immigrant, it was important for us to get together with others like us who shared a common culture. I have been cooking all my adult life and we probably averaged a party every two months for about twenty-five years. Besides, I had been catering for volunteer organizations for a very long time. One of my MBA projects was "How to Open an Indian Restaurant," and I remember that my marketing professor, Dr. Bose, liked it very much. When I look back on the project, it looks so simplistic because in reality, the bureaucratic, financial, and plain logistical problems that we encountered in opening a restaurant were a lot more than we anticipated. But thanks to my daughter's insight, we did open India Café, and it has been quite a journey!

A couple of weeks after we opened, a young man walked in. He came up to me and wanted to know the vegan items on the menu. Coming from India I was very familiar with the vegetarian diet. We have vegetarians of all kinds in India. Some of them eat eggs and yet many of them do not. Some eat only unfertilized eggs. Then there are the Jains, some of whom don't eat onions or garlic. They also do not eat vegetables that grow under the ground like potatoes. Sometimes they do not eat even vegetables that grow above the ground like tomatoes because tomatoes remind them of flesh! I did not know anything about being a vegan, and I had to ask him to explain it to me. When he explained it to me, I realized that a lot of South Indian vegetarian food was indeed vegan friendly. We do not have the extensive grazing lands like in the north of India that allow for easy availability of dairy products. And hence we had to contend with using coconut products to enrich our sauces and gravies. I also realized that the southern Indian diet was also gluten-free, because our main source of flour was chickpea and rice, both of which contain hardly any gluten. This gentleman who was a vegan is still a good customer of ours, and we have had a friendship that has lasted sixteen years.

One day I get a call from a secretary at Fort Gordon, which is the military base here in Augusta. An Indian general was visiting with his entourage, and they were having some high-level discussions at the Army base. The general was a Jain and hence a strict vegetarian, so they needed for us to cater a dinner that evening. For some reason, maybe because we were doing so much of the South Indian vegetarian dishes like masala dosa, idli, and oothappam, we had a reputation as a vegetarian joint. The catering chief that day was none other than my college freshman son who was home for the holidays. We had prepared a dinner of spinach pakoras and samosas for appetizers, kashmiri chicken and lamb rogan josh (for his non-vegetarian entourage as well as the Fort Gordon attendees), aloo gobi masala and chole' for dinner, and for dessert it was our signature mango cheesecake. My son, along with our waitress, left to do the catering, taking with him the food as well as the cutlery and crockery. Our dinner service at the Café' was in progress when I got a frantic call from Arjun who was overseeing the catering at the Army base. "Mom, is there any egg in the cheesecake?" OMG! We had thoroughly overlooked that! I had to tell him that there were indeed eggs in the cheesecake. When he came back he told us the rest of the story. The general was happy with the dinner after which he walked toward the cheesecake. He halted right in front of it and turned around and asked, "Are there any eggs in this cake?" My son was sure that his whole entourage was salivating over that cheesecake. But once the general declined it and walked back, all of them followed suit. Since then we had another order to make the same mango cheesecake without eggs for a Jain wedding. It was a bit of a challenge but we stabilized the cake with sour cream and a little bit more all-purpose flour. Our onion bhajias are vegan friendly, but they still might not meet the exacting rules followed by the Jains, who stay away from onions.

Onion Bhajias

Ingredients:

1 onion sliced into ¼ inch thick pieces

¼ cup chickpea flour (besan)

Salt to taste

1 teaspoon black cumin seeds

½ teaspoon chili powder

½ teaspoon of methi (fenugreek) powder

½ teaspoon garlic powder

½ teaspoon of ground black pepper.

3 tablespoons water

2 cups of vegetable oil to fry

In a bowl, whisk together the chickpea flour, salt, cumin seeds, chili powder, fenugreek powder, garlic powder, pepper, and water. Add the onions and mix well. In a wok, heat the vegetable oil to medium-high or 350° and drop the slices of onions into the oil, making sure that the onion rings are separated. Fry on both sides until golden brown. Serve it with the coconut chutney found in chapter 24. These can be great as an appetizer or as a snack for tea.

26

Star Struck: Tandoori Chicken

It seems to me that most of the lessons I learned in life were learned on some kind of steps—steps going up and steps going down. We were a group of about six girls—Girija, Radhika, Geetha, Ambika, my sister Deepa, and myself—who seemed to be constantly gathering on some kind of steps. Like when they built the steps leading up from the side of our house in the Koratty compound to the higher level of the swimming pool, many of us even penciled in our names with a twig on the wet concrete as soon as the workmen's backs were turned. That's how proprietorial we felt toward many of the steps in the compound. We gathered after school in the evenings and there was a definite hierarchy in the way we were seated. Since many of life's greatest lessons were being taught, usually the one with the greatest wisdom to impart sat at a higher level, and so on in descending levels. Sometimes the lowest rungs were occupied by wannabe groupies who were not yet old enough to join the group, and hence not fully able to comprehend the important subjects being discussed!

We sat there on those steps discussing crucial matters like movies and the age-old questions of where we came from. Girija was always the storyteller. In our small town we did not have access to the latest Hindi movies. But the clubhouse had a movie night every Wednesday where the kids got to see cartoons and National Geographic documentaries about animals and foreign places, and the adults got to see Western movies a couple of years after their releases.

My friend Girija always went to Cochin to visit her maternal grandparents over the weekend. Even in those days, Cochin was a thriving port city and metropolis. The latest movies and fashions came there. After each visit Girija would come back and tell us all about the latest Hindi movie she saw. She was a great storyteller, and I can almost picture her explaining a scene in one of these popular movies. "She looked so beautiful with her hair braided to the front and she was wearing just two small yellow roses. I'm telling you, when she smiled, the dimples were so pretty. And Rajesh Khanna, you could tell he really loved her by the way he was looking at her!" A bunch of imaginary moviegoers enthralled by the romantic scene that seemed to be happening right in front of them! My friend continued, "And after her husband died and her son had also become a pilot (the hero was doing double duty), she prayed so hard, with the Sari so tragically draped around her head, 'Please God, you took my husband, now do not take my son also!'" We were getting goosebumps listening to a story surrounded by such strong emotions. All things North Indian, we thought, were so much cooler than our own South Indian culture. So when

Girija's cousins came from Delhi, we thought they were the coolest kids. When we asked them about the latest Hindi movies we had only heard about, they would very dismissively wave a hand and say, "That is so old, yaar [buddy], have you seen his latest movie?" We felt like country bumpkins. Even the way they talked was so city-like—"yaar" this and "yaar" that. It was the start of the new "YAAR" fetish.

Another big preoccupation was how babies were made. Coming from the most conservative of southern families, with nuns as our educators, sex and childbirth were subjects . . . shrouded in mystery. For the longest time we were convinced that when a man and a woman kissed a baby popped out! So when we saw the older offspring of the English managers get together near the pool and sometimes casually kiss each other, we were horrified. We had seen our mothers stand around with shocked, disapproving expressions talking about servant girls who had gone astray and become pregnant out of wedlock only to bring, according to them, lasting shame on their families. We knew some funny business went on but did not have a clue as to the origin of the human species.

In one of these conferences on the steps, one enlightened person informed all of us that when a man and a woman kissed the woman's belly would grow bigger and bigger. Then when it was almost ready to burst, she would go to the bathroom and the baby would drop into the toilet, and the doctor and the nurse would hurriedly fish it out before it drowned. "Disgusting!" we all chorused together. How could a mother look at a child like that with such a loving gaze? Our friend sagely informed us, "That is a mother's love!" It certainly must be a love that transcends all sensory capacity!

We were always excited to go to a North Indian restaurant with its tandoori oven and see the chefs take out the red tandoori chicken on the long skewers. They would pat the soft dough discs onto the side of their mud ovens with such dexterity and courage (the tandoor burns at a temperature between 600° and 800°) and in a minute or two take out fluffy naans with their iron spears. There is definitely showmanship there, as well as a certain rustic charm. Only much later did it occur to me that many of the functions of a tandoor oven can be replicated in a modern oven with even better results. Some of the criticisms of a tandoor oven stem from the fact that it tends to dry out the meats, and sometimes the temperatures are not very even, resulting in uneven cooking where some parts might be burnt while other parts might not be cooked through. I have found a modern electric or gas oven with its grill pan to be ideal for the making of tandoori dishes.

Tandoori Chicken

Ingredients:

12 chicken breasts, deboned and skinned (washed and patted dry)

Salt to taste

1 teaspoon turmeric powder

½ a teaspoon chili powder

½ a teaspoon garam masala powder

½ a teaspoon methi (fenugreek) powder

1 teaspoon garlic powder

1 teaspoon ground black pepper

1 teaspoon onion powder

3 tablespoons tandoori masala

2 tablespoons apple cider vinegar

2 tablespoons vegetable oil

3 tablespoons plain yogurt (unsweetened)

In a bowl, mix the chicken with salt, turmeric powder, chili powder, garam masala powder, methi powder, garlic powder, ground black pepper, onion powder, tandoori masala powder, apple cider vinegar, vegetable oil, and yogurt. Mix it well and rub the masala onto the chicken (wear gloves if necessary). Preheat the oven to 350°. Pour 3 cups of water in the bottom compartment of your grilling pan. The top slotted layer should be sprayed down thoroughly with Pam. Place your chicken on the top layer of the pan in two neat rows. Place it in the oven and cook it for

40 minutes. At this time turn your chicken over to the other side and cook it again for 12 minutes. Your tandoori chicken is ready. It can be sliced and served over delicious salads or it can go into an exquisite wrap. It can also be served by itself in a dish of green peas to provide an eye-catching contrast.

27

Jumblees Medal: Banana Fritters

B y the time Sheefa, the third child in our family, was ready for school, Madura Coats had started its own school inside the compound in Koratty. The company built a brand-new, two-story building with the downstairs serving as the schoolhouse and the upstairs as the residence of the headmaster. The school had all the modern amenities and the curriculum followed was the Cambridge system. The lower classroom was in the charge of a young woman of Anglo-Indian heritage, and her name was Dorothy Rebello. She was a beautiful lady who wore all the latest Western styles of the '50s—polkadot, below-the-knee skirts with collar blouses cinched at the waist, and her hair was worn in a smart ponytail with bangs covering her forehead. My little brother and his friends adored her, and her helper for the younger class was an older Malayali lady by the name of Saramma. Now Saramma wore her native outfit called

Chatta and Mundu, which consisted of a white dhoti, the ends of which were made into the shape of a fan to be hung at the derrière in order to provide greater modesty. The chatta was a V-necked blouse with three-fourths sleeves made of the same material as the dhoti. Along with a small cheesecloth-like towel called the eerazhathorthe draped casually on one shoulder, this was the usual dress code for older Malayali country Christian women. Saramma probably had no education past the fourth grade, but she was very bright and had picked up quite a bit of English in a few years. You could see her taking a child who had been too industrious with the crayons or plasticine (playdo) to the washroom and explaining to the child, "Saramma washing, washing."

The uniform of the school was also unique. The management had decided that the uniform had to be practical to suit the hot Indian climate conditions. So the girls wore A-line dresses with straps, and the boys wore shorts and untucked shirts in the color of the school, which was a lighter green bordered by a darker green. They were also allowed to wear sandals to school. In the classroom for the older kids, each pupil progressed at their own pace, going through the different levels, and only the extracurricular subjects like art and music were shared. It was a novel concept very unlike the usual rigid Indian school system. But, amazingly, many of the pupils of the company school did quite well on standardized tests and college entrance exams.

The company brought in a principal from England. His name was Colin Page. He was a man in his 40s, fairly tall, balding, and was a cross between Maria from *The Sound of Music* and a strict English boarding school master. He would break out into song unabashedly and emphasized language and literature. Mr. Page, as we called him, showed a lot of leadership and was a great organizer. He was the one who started the Jumblees, a Scout-like organization not affiliated with any of the well-known children's organizations; it gave him tremendous flexibility to mold it to the particular challenges of our crowd and the local culture. Although my immediate sister and I attended the local convent school, Jumblees was open to all the kids in the compound who wished to participate. The dress code was informal, and the only uniform was a scarf worn around the neck. If I remember right, we convened usually on Wednesdays at 5 pm, (5 pm *sharp*, very British and very unlike Indians). The first order of business was to lineup in our various teams for inspection by Mr. Page. He would check our clothes and nails for cleanliness, and he would even look behind our ears! I could never understand why it was necessary to check behind my ears, because as Indians we wash our hair on a daily basis and go through copious ablutions. But I have been told that this is a common English fetish coming from an era where baths were not common. Most of us would have just come from school, hastily wolfed down a snack, and run up to the clubhouse for Jumblees. So it was not uncommon to see a kid with a nail cutter quickly trying to make his or her hands or feet more presentable to the judges. Upon inspection if someone had a point deduction for lack of cleanliness, the whole team took the hit!

During the one hour we spent at Jumblees every week, twenty minutes were devoted to learning some of the Scout-like activities, such as learning the different knots. We had to show proficiency in Reef Knot, Clove Hitch, and the like to earn the next level badge. He had interesting games like charades, memory tests, and poetry; he even tried his hand at teaching us how to do ballroom dancing with the help of Mrs. Capes. We laughed and giggled as both of them showed us the dance moves! But our very favorite activity always involved games. We did every imaginable kind of relay game, and sportsmanship was stressed in a big way. Jumblees did not discriminate between boys and girls, so it was refreshing, especially for the Indian girls, not to be restricted by the rigid norms of convention and modesty. In a wheelbarrow race, it was a common sight to see a little girl with her frock flying in the air being the wheelbarrow with a little guy holding her legs while she tried to move forward with her arms. My grandmother would have been shocked!

One of the badges to be won was for being a good host or hostess. In order to fulfill the requirements, the kid had to invite one of the adult judges to their home and go through the motions of a tea party. There is the art of welcoming a guest, setting the table, making small talk, and above all making two snacks along with a beverage, usually lime juice or orange squash. Mrs. Twadell, my judge, was a kind lady and easy to please. Mummy and I made four-inch small pancakes served with jam and an age-old Malayali favorite, banana fritters. These fritters are made with plantains that are so overripe that they will be black in color on the outside. My mother did the frying for me, but I was the one who did all the mixing and the dipping of bananas. Mrs. Twadell was very complimentary and was pleased to inform me that I had passed the test. Another badge down!

Banana Fritters

Ingredients:

4 overripe plantains (Remove their skin and cut each one in half. Then take each of the halves and vertically slice them in two.)

½ cup all-purpose flour

2 tablespoons rice flour

Salt to taste

¼ cup sugar

¼ teaspoon turmeric powder

1 tablespoon sour cream

1 tablespoon vanilla extract

1 teaspoon baking powder

Water as needed

2 cups vegetable oil for frying

In a bowl using a whisk, mix together the all-purpose flour, rice flour, salt, sugar, turmeric powder, sour cream, vanilla, baking powder, and water and make it into a batter a little thinner than a pancake batter. Dip the long banana slices in the batter, thoroughly coating them. Pour the oil into a wok at medium-high temperature, and when it reaches 350°, slide in the coated banana slices, making sure the wok is not overcrowded. When both sides become golden brown, take them out and lay them on a platter lined with paper towels. It should be soft like sweet caramel inside and crunchy on the outside. In Kerala, this is a common teatime snack that can be found even in the thatched-roof tea shops.

28

A Pittsburgh Steeler: Malabar Shrimp

During the first three years of India Café's operation, we used to offer a lunch in addition to dinner between 11 am and 2:30 pm. Later on, we went to a dinner-only model because it was starting to take a toll on me. Since I did all the cooking, I was at the café from 6 in the morning till midnight. We tried to train other cooks, but I was not very happy with the quality of personnel we were able to hire to work in a small café. So we gave up our lunch and concentrated on offering only dinner from 5:30 pm to 8:30 pm, Tuesday through Saturday. In this way I could stop at the supermarket on my way to work and still be able to start my cooking at the café around 11 am. It was mainly an office crowd, along with a few medical personnel, who constituted our

159

lunch crowd. There was an African-American gentleman who used to come for lunch and sometimes dinner with his wife. They were very pleasant, and he would always talk about bringing his son to our place. I remember that they liked the Malabar shrimp appetizer.

One day this gentleman and his wife walk in with a very young man, who was tall, lanky, and extremely polite. They sat at their usual table and proceeded to order lunch. They ordered shrimp and a couple of other dishes, and the couple enjoyed their meal. In fact, they told us so. But my waitress noticed that the young man was finding it a little spicy. Now our food is by no means very spicy; in fact, to many Indians who like things a little hot, we are positively on the mild side where spices are concerned. Many of them demand that the food be spiced up at least four levels higher. The young man kept asking for more and more water and was rubbing his lips because he felt the spices were burning him. In those days when we did lunch, we had our share of Army personnel, soldiers in their fatigues coming for a quick lunch. They would come in groups and were always full of laughter and fun and yet meticulously polite. The Army had indeed trained them well, and it was always "Yes ma'am, no ma'am," and no one could accuse them of not being courteous to the staff. There was a group of soldiers sitting at one of the tables, and there was big-time excitement among their midst. They kept looking toward the table where the young man sat, and they were beside themselves. In the end, many of the soldiers went over to the young man's table and started thumping him on the back and wishing him all the best.

I have never watched much American football. The few times I watched I could not bear it because it looked like when the players tackle, they inflict enormous pain on each other. I take my hat off to the physical strength and stamina that this must surely require, though. My waitress and I were watching with increasing interest at the open display of hero worship toward this young man. We could tell he was somebody. My waitress sauntered up to the soldier's table and casually asked them what all the excitement was about. It was then that we understood why his father, our customer, was eager for us to meet his son. He had every right to be extremely proud of him. The young man was none other than Mr. Arnold Harrison, at that time probably no more than twenty-five years old. He had been recruited by the Pittsburgh Steelers, and in his rookie year, he got to play in the Super Bowl because one of their players suddenly got injured and he had to step in. What a break for a young football player! I am sure Mr. Harrison went on to bigger things, but I'll always remember him as the sweet young man with such good manners who was so affectionate and gave me a big hug when we were introduced. Our food was a little spicy for him, but he was a good sport and was so genuine in the way he thanked me. In our hearts we always wish him well. The waitress did some quick thinking and got his autograph on a napkin which is still displayed proudly at India Café.

Malabar is the seacoast of Kerala where the fishing boats dock. The Kerala fishermen, because of ancient trade relations with China, have learned a fishing technique using a dragnet that is very typical of Oriental fishing. Growing up, we ate fish at least three times a week. Some were bought at the market while some of the smaller fish were sold by fishmongers who came to your back door on their bicycles with their baskets of sardines, mackerels, whiting, or mullets. Shrimp was at first considered to be a poor man's food and was fairly cheap. I remember my father ordering mussels by the dozens from Calicut for club parties. Nobody had much value for these sea creatures. They were also not in demand for another reason. Malayalees clean their shrimp and mussels very thoroughly. Each mussel is individually inspected and their stomach sack (the black looking part) is thoroughly excavated out, because people believe that eating it will make one sick.

Malabar Shrimp

Ingredients:

2 pounds of jumbo shrimp, shelled and deveined (washed and thoroughly patted dry)

1 onion chopped

3 garlic cloves, chopped

2 green chilies, chopped

Half a finger length of ginger, peeled and chopped

1 tablespoon chopped cilantro

1 tablespoon curry leaves

Salt to taste (very little salt is required for shrimp)

1 teaspoon turmeric powder

1 teaspoon chili powder

½ teaspoon (fenugreek) powder

1 teaspoon garlic powder

1 teaspoon ground black pepper

1 teaspoon onion powder

3 tablespoons coconut oil

Set a skillet over medium high, pour in the coconut oil, and add the onion, garlic, green chilies, ginger, cilantro, and curry leaves and stir until the mixture turns slightly brown at which time add salt, turmeric powder, chili powder, fenugreek powder, garlic powder, ground black pepper, and onion powder. Sauté it for a minute longer and add the shrimp, mixing the whole thing well. Turn up the temperature to the highest setting and keep the pan closed for about two minutes. Remove the lid and stir the contents well. Cook it for one more minute and your Malabar shrimp is ready. It is important not to overcook the shrimp.

29

Mutiny in the Hostel: Idli, Saambaar, Chutney

W hile in college some of us who came from other towns stayed in the hostel. The fees were very nominal since the nuns took it upon themselves as their mission to mold the minds of the young in a moral and spiritual way. We were in training to be model housewives, nuns, or if you wanted to be more radical, engage in professions like teaching, nursing, or medicine. One of my friends once described it as a jail! In return for sending us to this jail, our parents were satisfied that the nuns, being as strict as they were, would work on our minds for the sake of social conformity. The living conditions were sparse, but they always provided four meals a day, and although the convent kitchen could never be accused of being the Cordon Bleu, the meals were simple and wholesome.

After mass in the morning, we had a cup of coffee, and a typical breakfast would consist of something like idli, saambaar, and chutney. In the middle of our classes, we would come to the hostel for lunch at 1 o'clock and it was always rice with a meat or fish dish and a vegetable gravy. There would be a snack like banana fritters, vada (lentil donuts) or egg rolls (the soft malayali ones with the sweet coconut filling called "Muttachurul"), and chai at tea time. The nun in charge of the kitchen would have thought out our menu carefully for its nutritional content and also for its budget friendliness.

We ate rice for lunch and dinner. In any South Indian home, one of the biggest purchases is the massive quantities of rice every month. The poor people get subsidized rations of rice purchased in the government shops. This is to ensure that even those who cannot fully afford it would be able to get their basic minimum rice requirements. All the servants in our homes took advantage of this government scheme, and they paid hardly anything to purchase rice. The only problem with the ration rice is that sometimes it has an unpleasant odor to it. I do not know if it is from being stored in burlap sacks for a very long time in warehouses, or because it is just poor-quality rice. For some time we had been noticing when we entered the dining hall in the hostel, that there was a slight odor in the air. My friends Alicia, Ancy, and I would remark about it, and we kind of figured that the kitchen staff was mixing small amounts of the cheap ration rice with good quality rice in order to contain costs. It was a minor irritation, something we laughed about as we all sat together at the table talking over each other. We might tease a couple of servers who replenished the dishes and ask, "Ivide entha ithra mullappovinte naattam?" ("Why does the whole place smell of jasmine flowers?") These servers were usually poor women co-opted to work in the kitchen and hence they had a certain disdain for us privileged girls. They would sullenly pretend that they didn't hear us and turn away because they were on the management's side!

One evening we had finished the rosary and were coming down the stairs for dinner. The commotion of two hundred girls (women, maybe) coming down the wooden stairs is like the horses thundering down the tracks in *Ben Hur*. Even before we had reached anywhere near the dining room, the smell was unbearable. It literally smelled like an unwashed latrine! Everyone kept covering their noses with the ends of their saris. It was really that bad. Obviously the clever formula of ration rice to good quality rice had been tampered with, and someone either willfully or unwittingly had put more ration rice for cooking. Looking back, I think we felt more indignant than anything else that the establishment thought they could treat us in this demeaning way. There is always a last straw that leads even normally peaceable, giggling, carefree girls to suddenly sit up and say, "This is it, we have had enough!" Even now when I recall the events of that evening, it was like all our minds had converged into one, and we felt that it was time to march to the convent house a couple of yards from the hostel and register our complaint with the principal. All hell broke loose. We were banging our plates (luckily, they were steel plates) on the table and shouting slogans like we had seen the boys do, when they went on strike all the time at the engineering college across the street. It was all the more memorable because there had never been such an act of disobedience in the history of the hostel before or after. Girls who normally shied away from even standing up before the class to answer a question put forth by the professor were screaming like banshees as the procession headed towards the principal's house. "Kooooo, Kooooo!" we heckled just like our male counterparts, and when the principal emerged and tried to pacify and offer a vague apology, nobody was still satisfied. We heckled her too! The only way I can explain the events of that night is to say that times were changing, and women were more aware of their rights. It was probably a culmination of a lot of frustrations at being treated like schoolchildren. The next day the headlines in the local papers read, "Hostel Girls Go on Strike and Gheraoed [Detained] Their Principal! And All in the Name of Rice!" It was our very own Boston Tea Party! I am sure our dear brethren across the street in the engineering college were only too glad to inform the papers.

The quality of our meals certainly did improve, but all our parents were notified by the principal about our terrible behavior, and how she would welcome the opportunity to speak to them in person. Most of the parents ignored the letter, but my parents being the good citizens they were, came promptly with expressions like thunderclouds and had a meeting with the principal. My mother came away from the meeting and was really angry. Her main preoccupation was how she was going to get me married with a reputation as a strike leader! I can't think of a time before or after when I felt that sense of uninhibited liberation and freedom of expression as I did during our strike. In fact, as the years have gone by, I am rather proud of the fact that for once my timid friends and I stood up for ourselves and made it count!

Idli, Saambaar, Chutney

Ingredients:

1 cup urad daal (white lentils), washed and drained

1 cup long-grain rice, washed and drained

1 cup rice flour

1 cup cooked rice

2 cups water

1 teaspoon salt

Idli-making stand (available in all Indian grocery stores and can even be ordered on line)

Soak the urad daal and long-grain rice in water overnight. The next morning, drain the water and put them in a blender along with the cooked rice and 2 cups of water. We use a stone grinder at the café for grinding, but you can use a blender also. Grind it into a soft batter and add the rice flour. Add the salt as well and whisk it till the batter becomes smooth. Keep it covered in a warm place for about eight hours so that the batter is fermented. Pour 1 cup of water into a pressure cooker that is big enough for the idli-making stand. Put the pressure cooker on medium-high heat. Spray Pam thoroughly into the individual depressions of the idli stand. With a spoon, pour the fermented batter into each of the slots until it is filled all the way. Lower the stand into the pressure cooker, close the lid, and let it cook in the steam for 12 minutes. Do not put the weight on top of the pressure cooker. After 12 minutes open the lid and carefully take out the idli stand (it will be hot). Using a butter knife, you can slowly pry out the idlis from the depressions. Well-made idlis should be fluffy and soft. They are best served with saambaar (see chapter 20) and coconut chutney, which has been described in chapter 24.

30
India Café's Signature Brownies

Our brownies were famous even before we started the café six-teen years back. We baked them at Christmas for Sebastian's workplace, for our children's teachers, for innumerable charity fundraisers, and even to cheer up our friends when they were ill or depressed. It is one of the simplest of recipes and yet it has had the longest reach in terms of popularity and goodwill. I even bake them for many of our treating physicians, and their staff can recognize the rectangular aluminum foil pan arriving bulging with its delicious contents! They get so excited, and many of the administrative staff will ask my husband in anticipation, "Are those your famous brownies?" In our family, I think our kids are fairly indifferent to them, having grown up with brownies around all the time, but their spouses seem to like them a lot. The greatest use I found for the brownie was when I used to coordinate children's programs like drama and dance where I could use them as incentives to get the kids to practice!

My father was a great believer in introducing children to artistic endeavors, like public speaking and drama. He felt that the confidence children derive from standing up before an audience and giving a good account of themselves was invaluable. He was the one who always encouraged me to take part in elocution as well as extempore speaking. I remember my earliest stint as a speaker. It was at the district level (in India they are called Taluks) and it was on the occasion of the anniversary of Mahatma Gandhi's birthday. Annamma teacher was my school coordinator who came with me to the neighboring town of Chaalakudy. My always-supportive parents had also come along separately, and the plan was to leave for the weekend to my grandmother's house after I was finished with the speech. We were to speak on a subject regarding Mahatma Gandhi, and the topic would be given only five minutes before you went onto the stage. I was scared at many levels. I was one of the youngest competitors at twelve years of age, and some of the others were fourteen- and fifteen-year-old kids. Besides, I was the only girl in the competition! All the others carried extensive notes and kept murmuring lines of it to themselves. It was clear that they had a lot to say about any subject on the great man. They could rattle off points so fast it would make your head spin! I complained to my father, telling him I didn't think I would have more than five points that I could muster in five minutes. I told him how the others were so full of information that I would look stupid. He just reassured me and told me to speak slowly, enunciate all the words properly, and to look them in the eye when I spoke. It also did not help that I was the only one who was going to speak in English while the rest of them were going to wax eloquent in flowery Malayalam!

I was given some subject like, "Why do we refer to Mahatma Gandhi as "the Great"? Standing before the judges, my legs feeling like Jell-O, I tried to tell them in five sentences why I thought he deserved the title. I tried to remember all that my father had told me, and it paid off! I walked away with a gold medal that I still have in my possession.

The Augusta Malayali Association is a very active cultural organization. When our children were young, for twenty long years I was extremely active in organizing cultural programs for our young people. The motto of our organization was that no child who wanted to participate would be turned down. The result was that many of the dramas and little skits were written with specific kids in mind. Plays would have twenty-four characters with ages ranging from two to fourteen. I even had to learn how to sew because it would have been frightfully expensive to buy all the costumes required for such a vast crew. I can personally count at least twenty of these productions. Like my father, I am also a firm believer that participating in cultural programs is good for the full development of any child. If I had any hand in setting the present-day education curriculum, there are two areas in which I would bring about change. The school kids, irrespective of their backgrounds, should be given a breakfast, lunch, and supper in a bag to take home. Given the hectic lifestyles of most modern two-income working families, even among the so called "affluent," it does take a village to raise a child! Many a time, the nutritional needs of children are not addressed in the poorer or the better off families, and it should be dealt with at a national level. They should have more hands-on experiences with language and arts through participation.

While there was a lot of excitement on the day of the programs, the practices leading up to these could be tedious. So we went with a general rule. We were not looking for Bollywood perfection; it was more important that every child participate and be able to deliver a few lines. The result was that practices became fun and exciting. We would work on the play or dance for twenty minutes, and the next thirty minutes would be playtime! The kids would romp around our extensive yard playing catch, football, or plain goofing off on the golf cart. The more indoor ones would play Nintendo games. In between all this fun, they would run in and out of the kitchen, helping themselves to plenty of Coke, Kool-Aid, brownies, and chicken wings. I must say I enjoyed it as much as they did, and when their parents came to pick them up, it was a party all over again with the mothers taking tea and the fathers joining Sebastian for a glass of Scotch. Many of these youngsters are grown-up, responsible, professional adults, but many of them still have fond memories of their performing days. They always give me a warm hug whenever our paths cross. This brownie recipe is so simple as to be almost stupid, but it has given so much pleasure to so many people. The little brownie that could!

India Café's Signature Brownies

Ingredients:

3 packets of Hershey's triple chocolate brownie mix (available at Sam's)

3 sticks unsalted butter, melted

2 tablespoons vanilla extract

6 eggs

¼ cup of Nestlé's semi-sweet chocolate chips

In a bowl, empty the contents of the three bags of brownie mix, butter, eggs, vanilla, and chocolate chips. Wear gloves and mix them gently by hand. I generally do not use an electric mixer for this purpose because it is important not to over mix it. Heat the oven to 350°. In a rectangular cookie sheet sprayed thoroughly with Pam, spread the contents of the bowl evenly and bake for 27 minutes. Do not overbake. Let it cool on a rack for 4 hours and your brownie is ready to be cut with a pizza cutter. Lift each piece gently using a thin cake spade. As you can see, the brownie recipe is indeed very simple, but I forgot to mention the love that went with each piece. That must be why it tasted so special!

31

Stargazing and Aviyal

My friend Radhika was a lot of fun. Slender with delicate features and a beautiful singing voice, she was goofy and game for anything! We would sometimes ride together in her father's car to school because they had a driver. After school, we would roam around in the mango estates gossiping about friends, teachers, the new handsome bachelor trainees who had come to join the company, and anything else that would interest a young teenage mind. It was around this time that the compound was abuzz with news of a new female teacher who was coming from England to be the new principal of the Madura Coats School. Mr. Colin Page, the old principal, was returning to England, and it was with a lot of sadness that we watched him go. He had contributed a lot to the academic development as well as the social development of even the kids who were not in his school.

I first saw Miss Anne-Marie Bispham at one of the club gatherings. My siblings who were students at the company school had already met her, and they seemed favorably impressed. I think my first reaction was to think how young she looked! Tall, with a great body, she sported what I imagine every one of her generation in the Western world was wearing in those days: miniskirts, flowing midis, and daring shorts. She made it very clear right from the start that she met the world on her own terms. We were really intrigued. My friend Radhika informed me that she had heard her parents discuss the new teacher and heard that she was engaged to be married. In fact, if I remember rightly, she did sport a sapphire solitaire!

While Mr. Page concentrated on the literary side of education, Ms. Bispham's strength was in science and math. I remember her complaining about the unmitigated heat of the tropics. Her clothes were a constant source of discussion among our mothers. "A teacher wearing miniskirts, che', it is not a good influence!" was the collective view held by most of the Indian women in the compound. While our mothers spent a great deal of time on their silk and gold thread saris and had the goldsmiths make them the latest fashion in gold necklaces, there was an invisible boundary of modesty they would not cross. Very few of them would attempt to even wear a sleeveless blouse with the sari let alone a swimsuit. Even when our mothers played tennis (and a few really played well), they would wear a white cotton sari worn a little higher than usual. I wish I had photograph of them playing tennis in a sari!

Ms. Bispham was a thoroughly modern woman. She had female friends as well as male ones and she entertained both equally. Just like Mr. Page, her home was the apartment over the school furnished by the company. We would see her talking and laughing and sometimes lounging by the pool in her bikinis with some of the Scottish and Australian management trainees at the company. Looking back, it was probably very lonely for a young English woman in the backwaters of India, and she was glad to talk about things back home with people of like backgrounds. But this is where the Indian culture comes in. In India, especially in the 60s and 70s, most married women did not talk at any length with a man who was not her husband. Even male relatives were discouraged from talking to the women too much. The kitchen area where the women worked and where there were a number of servant girls present, was off-limits to all men.

So Ms. Bispham was intriguing to me and my little friend Radhika who grew up on a steady diet of Malayalam movies, which portrayed a betrothed woman as a cross between Mother Theresa and the Blessed Virgin Mary. If any man approached her, a Malayalam movie heroine would give this look of such disdain, enough to remind him that she was not that kind of woman! It was also to signal that any man who approaches a woman who was not his wife or daughter had evil intentions on his mind. We were sure that there were goings on in the upstairs apartments of the teacher!

One evening I was visiting Radhika in her house, and as usual her mother was pointing out some of her latest acquisitions in plants. Ammini Ammai ("ammai" stands for "aunty" in Malayalam and we referred to all of our friend's mothers as aunties) was a beautiful lady and, having a masters degree in botany, she was showing off a particular variety of orchid called the "Bethlehem Lily." Indeed, the inside of the flower did look like a small manger with baby Jesus lying in it. She was also a good vegetarian cook and went on inside to check in with her kitchen help as to how the meal was progressing.

Now, Radhika's house was diagonally across from the school-house. We certainly noticed that Ms. Bispham had some male company going up her flight of stairs. Our antennas were up, and our curiosity got the better of us. Radhika remembered the telescope that was her father's pride and joy, and she brought it out to the garden. Together we strained looking through it and adjusting the scope, trying to direct it toward the window on the second floor of the schoolhouse, which was about three hundred yards away. Alas! All we could see were shadows because of the wire mesh that every window was fitted with in order to keep away the mosquitoes. It was highly frustrating. At that time, Radhika's father Prasad Uncle (to most Indian kids even now, an older man or woman whether they are related to the family or not is an "aunty" and "uncle"), a genial man close to my father's age, came up the garden steps. He was back from work. He was so thrilled to see that we were showing an interest in his dear telescope. "Aren't the sky and the stars so thrilling?" he gushed, glad to see that we were budding astronomers. We grinned weakly and dismantled the telescope, putting it back in its place. I remember Ammini Ammai serving us a delicious dinner.

Aviyal

Ingredients:

2 green plantains washed, with the ends and ridges cut off, and julienned with the skin on

8 green beans, washed and halved

1 cup of cubed pumpkin (you can either buy the whole pumpkin and prepare it or you can get it in the frozen section of your grocery store)

1 cup of cubed winter melon (a white fibrous melon found in Indian and Asian grocery stores)

3 carrots, peeled and julienned

2 green zucchinis, julienned

2 yellow zucchinis, julienned

1 packet of frozen unsweetened grated coconut

9 shallots, peeled

3 garlic cloves

2 green chilies

1 finger length of ginger, peeled

Salt to taste

½ teaspoon turmeric powder

½ teaspoon chili powder

1 teaspoon black cumin seeds

1 teaspoon garlic powder

1 teaspoon ground black pepper

½ cup sour cream

3 cups water

6 tablespoons coconut oil

3 tablespoons curry leaves

In a blender, blend until smooth the frozen coconut, shallots, garlic, ginger, green chilies, cumin seeds, salt, turmeric powder, chili powder, garlic powder, ground black pepper, and 2 cups of water. Pour 1 cup of water into a deep saucepan, add a pinch of salt, and cook the plantains for 10 minutes on medium high. After five minutes, add the green beans and finish cooking both the vegetables for five minutes longer. When the 10 minutes are up, add the yellow and green zucchini, winter melon, pumpkin, carrots, and the ground mixture from the blender. Add the sour cream and stir everything well. Reduce the heat to medium low and cook for about 10 minutes. Before the last two minutes are up, add the coconut oil and curry leaves and give it one more stir.

This is a favorite mixed vegetable dish from Kerala that is served for all important Hindu festivals. The name "Aviyal" means a hodgepodge, and here it is a mixture of various tropical vegetables found in our gardens. In Keralite literature the term "Aviyal" is used to describe a messy state of things where nothing is distinguishable!

32
Plunger Art: Chili Ribs

erry and Regina are friends, and they come often for dinner
to India Café. They are both retired nurses about my age and
hence we struck up an easy friendship. They are both well dressed,
but Jerry has a style all of her own. My daughter always teases
me that my dressing style could be categorized as boho-chic. I
guess she is referring to all the native Indian tunics called kur-
tas that I wear in the summer, along with my artsy village silver
jewelry. These tunics made of cotton are extremely comfortable
in the summer, and besides, in the interest of conforming to the
majority, I am not ready to give up my Indian identity entirely,
although it has been forty-two years since I left India. I guess Jerry
is the same way. Being of African-American heritage, she loves
the native African prints, and is very striking with her elegant
high turbans that sometimes have a brooch pinned to it. Jerry is

tall like a model, so she can carry off her leopard-print top with leggings and chunky gold jewelry and look like she stepped out of a fashion magazine!

Jerry is also extremely talented in creative arts. She makes her own clothes, hats, and many times even the jewelry she wears. After proudly showing me a catalog of Anne Klein or Christian Dior, then pointing to one of the necklaces or bracelets depicted in the pages, she would show me her own recreation of the same work. They would look almost identical. While the designer brand would cost in the thousands, Jerry was able to replicate it probably with materials costing less than $50. She also repurposed hand-bags. Once when the local paper was dyed pink in honor of breast cancer day, Jerry took the newspaper and made the most beautiful bowler hat with it. Pink roses made of paper adorned the brim. To say she is creative is an understatement!

Jerry is always kind to me and would make decorations for the café that she would present to me when she came for dinner. At Christmas time, she took a discarded dressmaking Styrofoam dummy and made it into a beautiful Scarlet O'Hara look-alike, gown and all, with colorful Christmas bulbs and garlands of Christmas lights. That particular year it was our Christmas tree. It got a lot of attention, and Jerry was pleased.

A couple of months later, Jerry decided to make me another ornament for the café. She had taken a wig head (these are the plastic heads on which wigs are displayed), put makeup on the face using paint, and gave it a wig of curly hair. The head was inserted into the wooden handle of a plunger so that it could be displayed on a flat surface. She thought that it would look good at the entrance to the café like a welcoming face! Although I have every confidence in her art, a plunger with a Gothic face welcoming people to India Café . . . somehow I was not able to come to terms with that! I convinced Jerry that it would look best in my garden and she did not have a problem with it. So I took the plunger lady home.

Jerry was a big fan of our tandoori chicken wraps and Regina loved the lamb vindaloo. That was, until they discovered that I made decent ribs as well. At present their most favorite dish at India Café is the roasted ribs with chili sauce. Being a small café, I have very personal contact with my customers. Even as many of them walk in through the door, I know what they are going to order. My husband and I have known some of them for more than a decade! Like the very first customer who ever walked in through our door sixteen years back, I never knew the gentleman's name, but my waitress decided that he looked like a sea captain. So whenever he and his wife (I knew her name was Betsy; sadly, she died about eight years ago) came to dine, the waitress would inform me in the kitchen that the sea captain was in the café. Another customer is an eighty-five-year-old builder. He and his wife come occasionally, and since the gentleman also runs marathons, my waitress from rural Georgia would tell me that the "marathon grandpa" was in the house! We have had the opportunity to meet all kinds of people. One of the most inspiring ladies I met was a 103-year-old Italian wedding planner. They had come for the groom's dinner the night before the wedding, and believe it or not, she was in charge. As they were leaving the café, I had to ask her, "What is the secret of your health?" This woman who jumped out of an airplane at the young age of 99 promptly answered, "Keep moving, keep moving," and when the party was over, did just that by jumping up from her chair and going out the door, and briskly walking down the steps to the parking lot!

Ribs with Chili Sauce

Ingredients:

1 slab of pork baby back ribs (thoroughly rub salt onto them, then wash them and dry them with paper towel, this mild form of brining not only tenderizes the meat, but also gets rid of any gamey odors)

Salt to taste

2 teaspoons garlic powder

2 teaspoons ground black pepper

1 teaspoon onion powder

1 teaspoon garam masala

1 teaspoon chives

2 teaspoons sriracha powder

2 tablespoons apple cider vinegar

2 tablespoons soy sauce

1 tablespoon red hot sauce

3 tablespoons vegetable oil

Preheat oven to 350°. Place the ribs on a cookie sheet lined with aluminum foil and sprayed with Pam. Mix salt, garlic powder, ground black pepper, onion powder, garam masala, chives, sriracha powder, apple cider vinegar, soy sauce, hot sauce, and vegetable oil and rub it thoroughly on the ribs using your hands. Place the ribs in the center rack and bake for one hour. Then open the oven and turn the ribs so that the bottom side is on top. Cook it for another half hour. Turn the ribs one more time and cook for 20 minutes longer. They will be tender and come off the bones easily.

Chili Sauce

Ingredients:

½ onion chopped

2 green chilies, chopped

6 garlic cloves, chopped

1 finger length of ginger, peeled and chopped

3 tablespoons chopped cilantro

Salt to taste

2 teaspoons chili powder

1 teaspoon of garlic powder

1 teaspoon ground black pepper

1 teaspoon onion powder

1 teaspoon chopped dried chives

1 teaspoon chopped dried parsley

1 teaspoon crushed red pepper

¼ cup Worcestershire sauce

3 tablespoons apple cider vinegar

¼ cup soy sauce

3 tablespoons red hot sauce

¼ cup ketchup

3 tablespoons vegetable oil

3 tablespoons sesame oil

1 tablespoon of butter

3 tablespoons black sesame seeds

1 tablespoon cornstarch

2 cups of water

Place a saucepan over medium heat and pour in the vegetable oil, sesame oil, and butter. When it starts to get hot, add the sesame seeds. After a minute, add the garlic, onions, green chilies, ginger, and cilantro, and stir the mixture until it turns translucent. At this point add the salt, chili powder, garlic powder, ground black pepper, onion powder, chives, parsley, and crushed chili. Keep stirring. After a minute or two, add the Worcestershire sauce, apple cider vinegar, soy sauce, hot sauce, and ketchup. In a small cup make a slurry of the cornstarch and 2 tablespoons of water and add this to the saucepan. Also add the 2 cups of water at this time. Give it a good stir and reduce the heat to medium. Cook it for about five minutes until bubbles come up on the surface. At India Café we usually arrange the ribs on a platter and drizzle the sauce liberally on top.

33

The Halva Man: Bread Pudding

In the Trichur house front garden, where my paternal grandmother lived, a heated game of dodgeball (called Erupanthe) was going on. One of the elder grandkids would bring water in a kindi (a brass container with a long spout used like a pipe to pour out water during hand washing or cleansing in the bathroom) and draw the boundaries of the game by running with water flowing out of the kindi in a circle. There ended the rules. A throng of about twenty kids of varying ages from six to eighteen would take their places in the middle of the circle. There would be one kid who would start outside the circle with a ball. The idea was to throw it as hard as you could at someone in the circle and try to hit them somewhere between the neck and the ankle. Talk about unadulterated aggression let loose! The noise level was enough to give anybody a headache, and there would be constant arguing between the teams that the ball did not really make contact with the kid. We did not have the benefit of instant replay!

While all this commotion was going on outside, the adults—our parents and our grandmother—were playing cards inside for fairly high-stakes. It was the biggest pastime for the family, and they were all very good at it. If a hapless Vicar from the local church should decide to pay a home visit while they were playing cards, it was always fun for us kids to see how the grown-ups would hide the cards on the hexagonal table with the carved tiger legs and spread a nice white tablecloth over it. From the friendly smiles and the polite chatter, you could never guess that this churchgoing bunch were engaged in gambling just a few minutes ago! "Sukham alle Acha, kaappi kudikku." ("How are you, father? Please drink some coffee.") As soon as the unsuspecting priest's retreating form reached the main gate of the compound, off came the tablecloth, and they would resume their card game. The Casino was back in session.

As the kids played, sometimes you'd suddenly hear the loud cry of the halwa man. "Aluveeeee, Aluva! Badami Aluva! Veno, veno Aluva veno?" ("Halwa, halwa, halwa made with pistachios! Would you like some?") Now, Halwa is a North Indian dessert not commonly made in our homes. It is made by cooking down the gluten water taken from wheat along with butter, sugar, and in this case, pistachios. Chewy and sweet, most Indians love these sweet meats. Then the begging begins. The kids who were playing a minute ago would run inside and start pestering their parents, aunts, uncles, or whoever was susceptible to being convinced to buy them some halwa. Knowing that it was good business because of the huge number of kids, the halwa man would linger in front of our gate. He knew the kids would prevail. In the end, the unwritten rule among our grown-ups was that whoever was winning at cards treated all the kids to a piece of halwa! Upon getting the okay, the kids would be running to the gate inviting the halwa man to come down the steps with his sweet load.

He was a thin man with a gaunt face and a pointy chin. He always had a couple of days' worth of stubble on his chin. He would come carefully down the steps with this huge box the size of a cedar chest, with glass all around the sides in order to visually tempt people, balanced on his head. He would carefully place the heavy load on the veranda parapet, and all of us kids would swarm around just like the flies he was trying to flick off from his merchandise. There would be cashew halwas of orange color, pistachio halwas with their characteristic green color, and even the Kerala specialty, which is black halwa made with jaggery (brown sugar). We would all choose our various flavors, and he would take out his long serrated knife and cut pieces like he was cutting meat. He looked like he used the same knife to cut his hair too because his hair looked so jagged and uneven on his head. Everyone would try to stretch out the enjoyment by taking small bites and savoring every morsel. This simple pleasure was what I was trying to recreate when I started making our bread pudding.

Bread Pudding

Ingredients:

1 loaf of white bread

2 sticks of butter

1 quart half and half

2 teaspoon pumpkin pie spice

½ teaspoon nutmeg powder

¼ cup cashews, chopped

¼ cup raisins

4 eggs

10 egg yolks

1 quart heavy cream

2 tablespoons vanilla extract

2 ¼ cups sugar

½ teaspoon salt

Tear the pieces of bread into a rectangular cake pan sprayed with Pam and pour half the container of half and half over the bread pieces. With your hands, make sure all pieces of bread get wet. Pour in the melted butter, the cashews, raisins, pumpkin spice, and nutmeg powder. Mix all ingredients together with your hands. Break 4 eggs into a separate bowl and add ¼ cup of sugar, 1 tablespoon of vanilla, and the remaining half and half. Whisk the mixture by hand. Pour this half-and-half mixture over the bread and mix it thoroughly. Place it in a 350° oven for 1 hour, then inspect it to see if it has formed a crust. It will probably need to cook for another 30 more minutes for the crust to form.

In order to make the sauce for the bread pudding, separate 10 yolks from the eggs and place them in a bowl. Add the heavy cream, salt, 1 tablespoon of vanilla, 2 cups of sugar, and whisk it briskly. Pour this mixture into a double boiler and cook at medium heat, stirring constantly. After about five minutes you will notice that steam is coming off the stirring spoon when it is taken out of the liquid. The light-yellow cream will also coat your spoon and you can draw a line through it. This is how you know that your custard is ready.

At India Café, we usually warm up square pieces of bread pudding and pour 1 tablespoon of Captain Morgan's spiced rum on the piece. We then spoon a generous helping of the custard on top of it and finish it off with a dollop of whipped cream. It is a desert for the ages!

34

The Café Kids: Chicken Pakoras

Kids are so resilient. They adapt to anything life throws at them. I remember before going to school carrying our aluminum school boxes (in those days such boxes were all the rage; and we had pestered our father mercilessly until he relented and got them for us) there would be a customs inspection by Mom. There was a reason for this too. And I can assure you that it was not a drug check! My sister was a very enterprising young lady, and she would have gathered several pods of the dried-up tamarind -like fruit called Madras Eenthappazham (Madaras dates), which grew in profusion near the compound swimming pool. They were nowhere near as succulent as the real dates, but some of the young kids in school who craved sugar loved the stuff. My sister had a very good business reason for taking it to school. She would distribute it freely and there would be three or four kids busily doing her homework for her in return for a few pieces of the sickly sweet stuff. Talk about enterprising!

Our café has been in existence now for sixteen years, and we have seen so many young people come through. Like the two little girls who come with their dad to visit grandparents in town. They always split a chicken tikka masala, but their father swears that the real reason for their sudden interest in Indian food is the complementary brownie topped by a scoop of vanilla ice cream that I sent out, to be shared by two people at the table. I recall another young girl barely in middle school coming with her parents. She looked so delicate, and I did not think she could handle anything more spicy than grits, but she completely threw me off when she proceeded to order a masala dosa with its spicy saambaar and chutney. After many years we had the pleasure of one day welcoming her into the café sporting a beautiful diamond solitaire accompanied by a handsome young fiancé from South America.

I can still remember a young girl coming with her mother and grandmother and all of them proceeding to order chaat (crunchy street food appetizer), but what surprised us the most was when the little girl proceeded to order lamb vindaloo for herself as her dinner. The grandmother is no more, and the little girl has grown up into a beautiful young lady who is at present doing her masters in psychology in another state. I was most touched when a young couple came in with their newly adopted little girl, who at that time barely looked four, but was really six years old. She had been adopted from Chennai, India, and as soon as she saw me, I could sense that she felt a certain kindred spirit stemming, maybe, from a certain racial memory that we both shared. Her dark beautiful little face with its thick mane of hair and her thin arms and legs—she could have been any child I grew up with. She had shiny eyes and was insistent that she wanted to eat masala dosa; it was almost like a memory from her early childhood was prompting her. Her parents tried very hard to get her to try a little chicken, probably hoping to get some protein into her, but she was adamant about her masala dosa. Years later she came to the café with a young man. It was her first date!

But the most memorable of all of them were the librarian's daughters. Their mother, a school librarian, is a vegetarian, and hence had discovered our restaurant. She was a single mother at that time and would come in with her two daughters, and I must say these young ladies had very eclectic pallets! While their mother stuck to her vegetarian specials, the girls were game to try shrimp, duck, ribs, or anything else that I had put on special that day! Sometimes they came in with their father. The girls had plenty to talk about with both parents, and they would be vying with each other for their parent's attention. They were so confident and outgoing that they would strike up a conversation with me too, and that's how I got to know them really well. The oldest is now a working lady and the younger one is finishing up her masters. Even now when they come in and I hear the familiar "How are you, Priya?" it is like time has stood still. They would always start their dinner by ordering chicken pakoras. We get a very health-conscious crowd and they usually order a vegetarian appetizer and then maybe a chicken or fish main entrée. So while the chicken pakora is not one of our biggest sellers, we still keep it in honor of the little people who grew up with India Café!

Chicken Pakoras

Ingredients:

2 pounds boneless, skinless chicken thighs cut into small pieces

1 onion, chopped

2 green chilies, chopped

1 finger length of ginger, peeled and chopped

6 garlic cloves, chopped

3 tablespoons cilantro, chopped

3 tablespoons curry leaves

Salt to taste

2 teaspoons garam masala powder

2 teaspoons garlic powder

2 teaspoons ground black pepper

2 teaspoons onion powder

6 cardamom pods

1 stick of cinnamon

1 teaspoon of black cumin seeds

6 cloves

3 star anise

2 tablespoons soy sauce

2 tablespoons red hot sauce

1 tablespoon sour cream

2 eggs

1 cup all-purpose flour

1 tablespoon baking powder

2 cups vegetable oil for frying

In a coffee grinder, powder the cardamom, cinnamon stick, cloves, star anise, and cumin seeds. Then, in a bowl, mix the chicken, onions, garlic, green chilies, ginger, coriander leaves, curry leaves, salt, garam masala, garlic powder, ground black pepper, onion powder, soy sauce, hot sauce, all-purpose flour, baking powder, eggs, sour cream, and the coffee grinder mixture. Mix it well. In a wok at 350° (medium heat) on the stovetop, pour spoonfuls of the mixture and let it cook until brown. Make sure the chicken is thoroughly cooked inside. Chicken pakoras go very well with the green chutney (mentioned in chapter 17) or just plain ketchup or ranch dressing.

35

Vishu, the Hindu New Year:
Jackfruit and Coconut Ada

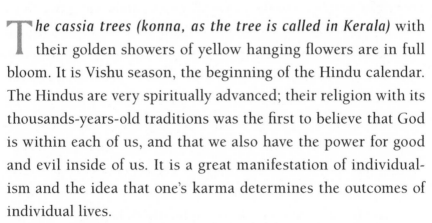

The cassia trees (konna, as the tree is called in Kerala) with their golden showers of yellow hanging flowers are in full bloom. It is Vishu season, the beginning of the Hindu calendar. The Hindus are very spiritually advanced; their religion with its thousands-years-old traditions was the first to believe that God is within each of us, and that we also have the power for good and evil inside of us. It is a great manifestation of individualism and the idea that one's karma determines the outcomes of individual lives.

As twilight approaches in a day, there is a beautiful custom that every South Indian Hindu household observes without failure. Each house will have its own dedicated room to the deity they worship whether it be Rama, Krishna, Shiva, or some other avatar of the great Creator Brahma. There are elaborate statues of silver, copper, and bronze, and every morning and evening fresh flowers would be offered along with bananas, coconuts, and jaggery. The puja room, as it is called, will always emanate a faint smell of incense burned at the altar. I cannot even count the number of times when I have heard Radhika's mother call out to her when we would get back after our evening sojourns around the compound. "Radhike," she would say, "poyi kulichittu velakku koluthi naamam jabikku!" ("Radhika, go and have your bath and light the sacred lamp in the puja room and worship the name of God!") One of the ways a Hindu prays is by reciting several different names of the same God, which glorify different attributes of the same Godhead.

On the morning of Vishu, the mother of the family would have gone to the prayer room and, having done her devotions, would then proceed to bring each member of the family into the puja room. She would close their eyes with her hands and guide them to the puja room, so that the first thing they would see (called the Kani) in the new year is the auspicious image of God. The kids love this festival because it also involves Vishukkaineettam, the custom of the adults giving the children money as a blessing so that they will be successful in a worldly way as well. This is a festival celebrated mainly in Kerala, and every household has its traditional dishes that they prepare. The schools get a few days off, and we would spend those days in my maternal grandmother Thresia's home in Mattom. My grandmother's help Kaali and her friends in the village would be so excited. This village was, according to our modern civilized standards, extremely backward. Many of the women over the age of forty did not wear anything to cover their breasts. Looking back, they had a lot of similarities to many of African tribal peoples.

There is the famous story about how my father who, like most men of his generation, never stayed even for a day under the roof of his mother-in-law (this was easy in the days of the arranged marriage where the marriages involved families within a ten-mile radius), had sent a suitcase to be given to my mother and had entrusted it to his nephew, a young man of about twenty years of age. This was the first time my paternal cousin had visited the countryside where my maternal grandmother lived. He got off the bus and was standing there with a suitcase wondering which direction on the dirt road he had to take to reach my grandmother's house. Along comes Kurumbathalla, an ancient, wrinkled old woman with her pendulous breasts swaying as she walked! She asked him, "Mon evadekka pone?" ("Where are you going?") My cousin told her the family he was interested in and she said, "Judgeede veettilekka, enda koode pore!" ("Oh, to the judge's house? Come with me!") With that, she hoisted up the suitcase and walked in front of him with her breasts in tow, and this was how we saw my young cousin sheepishly walking toward my grandmother's front door! As you can imagine, we never let him hear the end of it. My grandfather was a lawyer and not a judge, but to a villager it was all the same.

The tribal villagers had their own customs, and we kids were allowed to go with my grandmother's help Kaali and watch the celebrations in front of their mud huts. The men would be in high spirits on the local toddy, and I suspect the women were helping themselves to it as well. In rhythmic steps they would go round and round, their bare feet pounding the dry baked cow-dung coated earth in front of one of their homes. "Enda thumbi thullathe!" (a song egging on the butterfly to dance) they would chant, dancing in a circle. Soon one of the ladies (I guess one of the more impressionable ones) with her hair streaming in the wind and a wild look in her eyes, would work herself into a frenzy with jerky motions of her hands and her head wobbling at the same time. We kids watched it with horror and yet with a strange fascination. The climax would come when she would finally fall to the ground in a trance!

Jackfruit and Coconut Ada

Ingredients:

4 cans of ripe jackfruit flesh (usually available in Indian and Asian markets)

1 cup water

2 cups rice flour

Salt to taste

1 packet of unsweetened grated coconut

1 cup brown sugar

1 teaspoon cardamom powder

Fresh or frozen banana leaves (these are available in Mexican stores)

Cut the jackfruit into little pieces and put it in a pressure cooker with 1 cup of water. Close it and put it on the stove at medium heat. When the pressure starts to come out at the top, put the weight on and cook for 25 minutes. In a bowl, put the rice flour, salt, and the jackfruit with the hot water. With a spoon, mix it thoroughly. Cut the banana leaves into 10" x 5" rectangles. In another bowl, mix the coconut, brown sugar, and cardamom powder. Take a small ball of the rice dough and place it in the middle of one of the banana leaf rectangles. Wetting your hand with a little water, spread the dough in a thin layer on the leaf. Take a good spoonful of the coconut mixture and put it in the center of the dough. Fold the leaf over so that the whole thing looks like a purse and the dough and coconut filling are inside. Take some water in a big pot, place a colander in it, and put it on the stove at medium heat. Place the adas in it and cover with a lid. Steam for about 20 minutes. It is one of the best teatime snacks. (My grandmother probably never saw a can of jackfruit. It grew in her garden in abundance. When the jackfruit was green it was used as a vegetable and when it ripened, it would be used in snacks or desserts.)

36

The Rookie Reporter: Erissery

It was around 8:15 pm, and things at the café were winding down. The phone rang and the person at the other end wanted to know if he could come to dinner in about five minutes. We usually stop seating at 8:30 and so my husband informed him that he could still seat him. That day was the beginning of a friendship between an exceptional young man and us.

He came bounding in as he always would, full of energy and enthusiasm. He was about my daughter's age. From his name, I could tell that he was a Brahmin from the Tamil Nadu-Kerala border regions. Archith Seshadri was working as a young reporter for the local ABC affiliate here in Augusta, Georgia. He is an engineering graduate from Georgia Tech and this knowledge gave him a great deal of advantage in reporting, especially when he had to report on very technical subjects, such as happenings in the nuclear power plants nearby. He had mentioned to us that his father, a successful Engineer from India was disappointed that his son had chosen journalism, which was not considered one of the more desirable professions among the Indian educated elite. But the young man was passionate about his work, and his dedication, industriousness, and willingness to learn certainly paid off!

Archith went on to become a primetime anchor in New Delhi, India, for a global English network. It tickled me to no end when I was in India visiting my family that when the TV was turned on to global news, a familiar face was the anchor. Since then he has come back and is the Atlanta bureau chief for the Nextar Media Group representing four TV stations and 45 counties in Georgia. He appeared on ABC's *$100,000 Pyramid* with Snoop Dogg and Questlove and was a winner! Archith is also a foodie who tries out just about every restaurant in town and loves to cook himself. Being a strict vegetarian is what attracted him to our café in the first place, and he seemed to enjoy all the usual fare—chole (garbanzo beans), green beans thoran, and saambaar. He told us that his mother cooks many of the dishes native to Kerala since they derive their heritage from both states, Kerala and Tamil Nadu. He would get particularly excited when I made the festival dishes of Kerala like Erissery, which is a mix of black-eyed peas, pumpkin, and coconut.

Legumes have long been the backbone of Indian cuisine whether it is black-eyed peas, field peas, daals (lentils) of every variety, or garbanzo beans. For most ordinary Indians, a bowl of rice and a curry made of some legume is a full meal by itself. The farmers eat this meal and so do most of the working classes in India. Anything over and above this is a luxury. When I started the café, it was interesting to me that this everyday vegetarian dish was proving to be a popular item with my American clientele.

Archith still keeps in touch; that is one of his most endearing traits. Periodically I see pictures of him trying out different exotic, ethnic foods all over the world (all vegetarian of course), and I can almost see him eating and working at the same time, checking on his sources and gathering information for the next day's newscast. And through it all he would be complimenting the food and thanking us profusely!

Erissery

Ingredients:

2 cups dried black-eyed peas washed (immerse it fully in water for eight hours before cooking)

2 cups cubed pumpkin (cubed butternut squash is a good substitute)

Salt to taste

6 shallots, chopped

6 garlic cloves, chopped

2 green chilies, chopped

1 finger length of ginger, peeled and chopped

3 tablespoons curry leaves

1 packet of frozen unsweetened grated coconut

1 tablespoon black cumin seeds

2 tablespoons black mustard seeds

4 dried chili pods

2 teaspoons turmeric powder

2 teaspoons chili powder

4 teaspoons coriander powder

1 teaspoon ground black pepper

1 tablespoon tamarind pulp

1 tablespoon sour cream

4 tablespoons coconut oil

Place the drained black-eyed peas in a pot with 2 cups of water and salt, and cook for 15 minutes. The black-eyed peas will be tender. Pour the coconut oil into a saucepan over medium-high heat, and when it is fully heated, add the cumin seeds, mustard *seeds, dried chili pods, and curry leaves. When the mustard starts popping, add the shallots, garlic, green chilies, grated coconut, and ginger, and sauté it until golden. Add salt (if necessary), turmeric powder, chili powder, coriander powder, and ground black pepper and sauté for one more minute. Add to this the pumpkin, tamarind pulp, sour cream, and the cooked black-eyed peas and mix well. Cook at medium heat from 7 to 10 minutes until the pumpkin is tender.*

37

Dress Rehearsal:
Mango Colada and Spinach Pakoras

It is ironic that my very first dance teacher was a Muslim lady called Jamila. She was a short, petite woman with eyes lined heavily in Kohl and a long tail of Kohl streaming Cleopatra style from the tips of her eyes. She always came to the house to teach my sister, me, and some of the neighboring kids. Sometimes she would show my mother her swollen ankles from a previous night's performance, where she would have worn heavy ankle belts made from felt, with sixty heavy bells sewn onto it, in order to beat out the rhythm of the music. I can't say we appreciated all this because it just seemed an unnecessary intrusion into our playing time. As soon as we came near the house and saw her sitting there waiting for us, I would start, "Mummy kaalu vethana avunu!" ("Mummy, my leg is hurting!") My mother would have none of that nonsense! But it started an involvement in dance, music, and drama that I enjoyed even until 2004. The sad part of it was that when I finally started getting interested in classical dancing, and even the nuns who were my teachers were recommending that I take lessons, my mother's Catholic inhibitions came to play. She felt that if I took formal lessons and performed in formal venues, it would be too much "exposure." In the India of the 70s, mothers were still more preoccupied with the girl's eligibility in the marriage market.

However, my mother was always encouraging my sisters and I to participate in cultural programs whether at school, college, or community level. As a twelve-year-old, when we used to spend part of our long summer vacation at my maternal grandmother's house in Mattom, the nuns of the local school would invite me to teach some of their school kids a couple of dances so that they could perform at the annual day for the village school. There were no playback singers, no orchestra, and no piped-in music. We sang as we danced with maybe one microphone on a stand on the stage. I begged my mother to lend me one of her saris to drape myself as I had seen the movie stars wear; in short, it was extremely home-spun to say the least. And yet those villagers had gone to a lot of trouble to put up the show. There would be a raised stage with a thatched roof and benches for the audience to sit on. At dusk they would come walking from all corners of the village and the hills near Mattom, carrying fiery torches made from dried coconut leaf bundles, and you could see them swinging these torches so that they don't burn out!

I still believe that being involved in local cultural activities brings out the most creative elements in a person. When my husband's job brought us to Augusta, Georgia, we got involved in the local Malayali Association of people from Kerala, and we have had a lot of fun doing various activities like dancing and drama for the adults as well. It brings back so many memories. We are rehearsing for a play written by our very own playwright, Thampi, and we are going over our lines. The venue is the home of our dear friends, Paul and Indira, who are also in the play. The storyline is about a young immigrant man from Kerala played by Thampi himself. He goes back to India to get married in the arranged marriage way. Paul is playing the marriage broker's part, and Georgie and I are the girl's parents. The prospective bride is played by none other than Thampi's wife in real life, Thresiamma. There is a scene where the broker (Paul), pinches the prospective groom (Thampi) in the butt, when he gets too fresh in his first interview with his prospective bride (Thresiamma). Being the compulsive playwright that he is, Thampi would make Paul pinch him every time that line came up! It was enough for the cast and crew to get a bellyache from laughing.

Another time when we were doing a pantomime on stage as Mahatma Gandhi and Subhash Chandra Bose (two freedom fighters), the part of Bose was played by Thampi. He noticed that Mahatma Gandhi's dhoti was slowly slipping. With a flourish, he pinned it up for Gandhi like it was all part of the grand scheme of things, and the audience roared! Then there was the time we attempted a grand Dickensian Christmas production with an aging couple as our lead. The sari lends itself to any kind of costume you want to turn it into. It can be worn like a village lady in India, or it can be draped like the old-style British gowns. The lead couple was having trouble with their lines, and this was when we discovered the art of lip-synching. All of us walked around in our grand costumes trying to keep our lips in sync with the tape recorder! For another play,

Ashok was our prompter. The actors were having trouble hearing his prompting over the hum of the audience, and he had to keep raising his voice so that we could hear him. Toward the end of the play, even the audience could hear him loud and clear!

We made rehearsals into a fine art. We would gather in someone's house and there would be drinks, short eats, and sometimes dinner. The rehearsals were more fun than the actual performance itself. We ate and drank and laughed at ourselves, and in the end it was shared camaraderie among people who grew up in a certain culture and were finding delight in transplanting it ten thousand miles away from their towns and villages in a little state called Kerala.

Mango Colada

Ingredients:

1 can of Alfonzo mango pulp

1 can of cream of coconut

2 scoops of vanilla ice cream

3 cans of sprite

1 jigger of Capt. Morgan's spiced rum

In a blender, mix all of the above and serve it in a chilled tall glass kept in the freezer, preferably with a little cocktail umbrella.

Spinach Pakoras

Ingredients:

2 lbs fresh baby spinach, cut up

1 onion, chopped

2 green chilies, chopped

1 finger length of ginger, peeled and chopped

3 tablespoons chopped coriander leaves

3 tablespoons curry leaves

Salt to taste

2 teaspoons chili powder

2 teaspoons ground black pepper

2 teaspoons garlic powder

½ teaspoon methi (fenugreek) powder

1 tablespoon black cumin seeds

1 small packet of frozen green peas

2 cups of besan (chickpea) flour (available in Indian stores)

¼ cup all-purpose flour

1 tablespoon baking powder

2 eggs

1 tablespoon sour cream

1 cup water

2 cups vegetable oil for frying

Mix all the ingredients together in a bowl with the one cup of water. In a wok, heat the vegetable oil to medium heat (350°) and drop in spoonfuls of the spinach batter and fry it until golden brown. It can be served with a mint chutney (chapter 17) or ranch dressing.

38

The Quail Trapper: Ammamma's Quail Fry

W*hen my maternal grandfather was a practicing lawyer* in Madras (again, it was Madras in those days, not Chennai), almost every vacation was spent there. We went by train or car and had the best time with my grandparents, uncles, and aunt. All through the day we roamed round the spacious compound and gawked at the school kids in the compound at the back of our grounds. At the crack of dawn, the milk service began. The milking cow along with its owner would enter the gates of our yard and wait. The caste system was definitely at work here. The owner would have been a person of a lesser caste and hence he could not milk the cow himself although he owned the cow! That privilege belonged to a so-called cleaner, higher-cast person who would come very officiously, wash the udders of the cow, and begin milking; you could hear the sweet milk falling in a fierce stream into the aluminum container. This was the daily milk run. Having no grocery stores with shelves stacked with milk cartons, this was the only milk available for the rest of the day.

After breakfast was over, Ammamma (as we called our grandmother) would direct her attention to what she wanted to cook for lunch. The vegetable sellers would be calling their wares on the street just outside our windows. Chicken was grown outside the house, and it was used mainly when company came. Mutton and beef (beef was rare because Madras was a very Hindu town and cows were not usually slaughtered) were available only in the Moor market or the other small-city markets. This would require my grandmother to take a rickshaw pulled by a man, and sometimes I was taken along when she visited the markets. If I behaved myself, she would reward me by buying a small set of clay pots and pans for me to play with.

Another person of great interest to us kids was the quail seller. He would come in the gates wiry and thin, his white dhoti and shirt a stark contrast to his charcoal skin. There would be a long bamboo pole on his shoulder and on one end of the pole would be hung what looked to us like a wide reed basket. Even before he came in through the gates you could hear his cry along the street: "Kaada, kowdaari, kaada, kowdaareeee!" ("Quail and partridges!") And my grandmother would ask the servant to call him. There would be so many little birds chirping around in his basket, which was actually a trap set out for them! Then would begin a serious round of haggling. My grandmother would offer him ₹0.25 for twelve quail, and he would reply that his family was starving and he did not plan on giving away his birds for free, To which my grandmother would come back with a look toward the servant: "Why did you let this robber in if he is planning on cheating me blind?" I think it kept everyone entertained. In the end my grandmother would have purchased enough quail to feed everyone, and the price quoted would require the quail seller to skin the birds for her. It was amazing to watch the dexterity with which he could perform this task. He would put Morimoto to shame!

My grandmother did not have an oven and hence she had to rely on marinating the quail first, and then frying it in a big open vessel called the "urili." After frying, she would pour in some water or coconut milk, close the lid, and cook it until tender. I propose to do this in another way so that the quail comes out crispy and crunchy.

Evenings in Madras were pure joy. Occasionally my grandmother would get us all dressed up, and we would pile into my grandfather's Morris Minor and visit other families. This was not as much fun for us kids because we had to mind our p's and q's. What we loved the most was when our bachelor uncles came back from work and entertained us by taking us on the backs of their scooters at breakneck speeds on the main roads of Madras. They were young, unattached, and sported Elvis hairdos and Beatles pants.

Many an evening we walked to the end of Sullivan Street and cut across the main road with San Thome Cathedral on the other side leading to Marina Beach. I wonder if I can still find my baptism registration at the Cathedral. Madras was a very fashionable city, and everyone coming to the beach was dressed so beautifully. The Western crowd would wear the high fashions of the day with their hair brushed to perfection and let loose, while the more conservative ones would wear their beautiful saris and long braided hair, often adorned with mullappoo (jasmine) or kanakaambaram (firecracker flowers). The sound of laughter and bangles jingling along with the heady smell of flowers lingered in the air. There would be a man selling ice fruit—his cry of "iiiiice prooot, iiice proooot!" could be heard everywhere—and many a time we could get the adults to indulge us with an ice fruit. The flavors were simple. It was either frozen sugared milk, or some variation of sugar and citric acid flavored and on a stick. But to a kid it was a real treat, with the sugary mess running down your hand while you cooled your tongue by licking it.

Ammamma's Quail Fry

Ingredients:

Four quail dressed, washed and patted dry

Salt to taste

2 teaspoons Chinese five spice powder

2 teaspoons garlic powder

2 teaspoons ground black pepper

1 teaspoon of onion powder

2 teaspoons dried chopped chives

1 teaspoon of lemongrass powder

2 tablespoons olive oil

1 tablespoon soy sauce

1 tablespoon Sriracha sauce

3 cups vegetable oil for frying

In a bowl, mix together the salt, five spice powder, garlic powder, ground black pepper, onion powder, chives, lemongrass powder, olive oil, soy sauce, and the Sriracha sauce. Rub this mixture on the quail inside and out thoroughly. Heat the oven to 350°. Pour 2 cups of water in the bottom compartment of your broiler pan. Spray Pam liberally on the top slotted pan of your broiler pan and place the quail on it. Cook it in the oven for 45 minutes. The quail will be cooked thoroughly. In a wok heated to medium-high heat, pour in the vegetable oil and when the oil reaches 350°, add the quail and fry it until golden brown. This is a wonderful accompaniment to many a cocktail!

39

Convent Romance: Cholé

I t is vacation time again in the big Trichur house where my
paternal grandmother lived. It is about 9 pm and the adults are at
their usual card game in the main parlor of the house. In the dining
room, off to the side of the kitchen wing of the house where about
twenty grandchildren are gathered together, there is an ancient
Catholic ritual being conducted. At nighttime we were all issued
a mat, a pillow, and one thin flannel blanket each. The girls slept
in one hall of the house, the boys slept in the main parlor, and the
adults occupied the bedrooms upstairs. My grandmother's room
was on one side of the parlor. My cousin Jope, who was about sixteen at this time, was conducting high mass, ably assisted by Elsy
Auntie's son, Raphael (we have to distinguish between the various
Raphaels, because I have at least eight cousins named Raphael,

after my paternal grandfather). Jope had draped his blanket around him and was holding up one of the coveted trophies won by my father and his brothers in football. He had helped himself to my grandmother's orange squash (as I mentioned before, we called all juice "squash"), which she served to the guests. He also knew where she kept the special cookies for company, the ones she hid in her huge wooden chest used to keep several hundred kilograms of rice. All the girls used their blankets to drape around their heads like the nuns.

It was time for Holy Communion. Father Jope raised his trophy chalice and muttered, "Amen, Kantheesho, amen Kantheesho," trying to imitate the priest during mass (being Syrian Catholic, the mass then used to be said in Syriac which none of us understood). We nuns lined up with pious attitudes, and Jope would dip one fourth of a cookie into the orange squash and put it on our tongues while muttering more rubbish. Then it was time for the leftover communion to be consumed by the priest in one swell swig. Suddenly all hell broke loose because the nuns felt that the priests had kept the lion's share of the communion wafers (cookies) for themselves and we were not going down without a fight. The holy wars of history had nothing on us!

As girls, our lives were dominated by nuns and we had a kind of love-hate relationship with them. In high school, if there was a pretty nun who taught us, there would be a rumor going around that it was because her mother had taken a vow at her birth to dedicate her to the church (even if it was against her wishes). This tragic tale would bring on sympathetic glances directed at the nun from her young pupils. If a nun was particularly unattractive, we thought she must have become a nun because her father could not afford the exorbitant sum he would have to pay as dowry to marry her off. I guess this was sad too! Teenagers have a way of making any tale into a Romeo and Juliet story.

Then there was our political science professor, a nun of such remarkable beauty that she looked like a medieval heroine. As she would walk the hundred or so yards from the college to her convent, our always-helpful brethren studying at the engineering college opposite our women's college would be lined up on top of the wall yelling to her at the top of their voices, "Enthina, Sister, ee athyahitham cheythathe? Ennodu paranja mathiyayirunnille, njaan vannu kalyanam kazhichene!" ("Why did you do this terrible thing, Sister? If only you had just mentioned this to me, I would have married you myself!") This is what she had to endure on a daily basis.

We had some really great educators who were nuns. I still remember Sister Perpetua from my middle school and Sister Lisia, the principal of my high school. Sister Stella Maria, the principal of our college, as well as Sister Cleopatra who was the head of the English department, and her assistant Sister Crysaloga were all nuns with remarkable character and integrity. I would be remiss if I did not mention some of the petty ones as well. Our hostel warden was a professor in Hindi, though her first love was math. Despite that, she was resigned to teaching Hindi because the college needed a professor in that subject. Her accent was terrible and her attitude toward her wards in the hostel was hostile, to say the least. She was great friends with this other nun who was a physics lecturer in our college. Together they would sit chatting and if any hostel student walked by, they would have plenty of comments about their manner of dress. "Why is your blouse so small at the back? Why is your sari worn showing so much of your stomach?" On and on it went, irritating the young ladies to no end!

One day when I arrived in class, the class was all abuzz with the latest gossip. The hostel warden's nun friend had run off with one of the engineering college boys! She had had a clandestine love affair with him and decided to cast off her habit. You think we were going to waste this golden opportunity after all the criticisms we had endured? Some of our students saw her waiting for the bus on the main highway along with her new husband, and they were quick to pounce, saying, "Alla ithu Sr. Saavitt alle? Sukhamaano?" ("Oh, isn't this Sister Saavitt? Are you doing well?") They reported that she had on a blouse that was even shorter than our fashionable ones, and so they could not resist commenting on it: "Blousu nannayittundu tto, korachu cheruthaa, pakshe, sarallya!" they said. ("Your blouse looks good, a little small but that's all right!") And they had the satisfaction of seeing her slink away in a hurry.

Any association with the hostel brings back memories of eating legumes till they came out of our ears. We had some type of legume for the afternoon and evening meals and the supply never seemed to deplete!

Cholé (Garbanzo Beans)

Ingredients:

2 cups of dried garbanzo beans, washed and drained. Soak them in water for 8 hours before cooking.

1 onion, chopped

6 garlic cloves, chopped

3 green chilies, chopped

1 finger length of ginger, peeled and chopped

3 tablespoons coriander leaves, chopped

Salt to taste

1 tablespoon black cumin seeds

2 teaspoons turmeric powder

2 teaspoons chili powder

4 teaspoons coriander powder

4 teaspoons garam masala powder

½ teaspoon methi (fenugreek) powder

1 small can of tomato paste

4 cups water

1 stick of butter

In a pressure cooker, place the drained garbanzo beans along with salt and 3 cups of water. Close the lid of the pressure cooker and set it over medium-high heat. When the steam escapes at the top, put the weight on and continue cooking for 15 minutes. This will make the beans tender. In a saucepan at medium high heat, melt the butter and add the cumin seeds, onions, garlic, green chilies, ginger, and cilantro leaves. When the mixture becomes translucent, add the turmeric powder, chili powder, coriander powder, garam masala powder, and the methi (fenugreek) powder. When this starts to brown, add the tomato paste and one more cup of water as well as the cooked garbanzo beans with their water and give it a good stir. Cook it for about 5 minutes until bubbles appear at the top. It is great with naan or rice.

40
A Gardener's Tale: Rabbit Stew

The very last house we stayed in at the Koratty compound of Madura Coats where my father worked was a beautiful bungalow facing a vast expanse of gardens with mango trees everywhere. The lawns were emerald green and the beautiful flame of the forest tree spread its fiery red canopy, kindly offering shade from the relentless sun. The gardener, a small man with thin bowed legs, would squat in the grass and trim the lawn with the long sword-like scythe in leisurely slow motion. I had never seen that man do anything in a hurry. One day his wife, who was twice his height with a big bun on top of her head and wearing a sari that seemed too short for her tall figure, sauntered up to him to ask for money. "Korache kaashe venam (I need a little money)," she said, flirtatiously. "Ninakkendinaa kaashe (what do you need the money for)?" our hero asked, with a leer. "Ari vedikkaana (it is to buy rice)," she replied. They were a spicy couple. Their interactions always had an edge that as a kid I could never fully comprehend.

When our mango trees were brimming with ripe mangoes, my mother would make "maanga thera," a kind of super-sweet mango jerky. The mango pulp from each day's supply of ripe mangoes would be spread out on a thin reed tray called a "moram." This is put out in the sun to dry. The next day another layer of mango pulp would go on top of it and again it was left out to dry. This went on for several days, after which you get a bark with several layers of sweet mango. It is a big favorite in Kerala. My mother was very proud of her mango bark that was coming along with many layers.

One day when my mother was working in the kitchen, the gardener came running in very distraught and informed her that he saw an "arana" (garden lizard) running across the mango tray that had been kept out on the concrete driveway to dry! My mother was beside herself, but she was also very scared that the tray had been poisoned because in Kerala the proverb is that "Arana kadichaal udane maranam!" ("If the garden lizard bites you, you will drop dead immediately.") Only much later, after I came to America and I saw little kids catching these lizards, did I realize that they were perfectly harmless! But my mother was in a dilemma as to what to do. "Throw it out immediately," my father thundered. My mother's heart broke as the gardener carted away her precious mango bark, supposedly to throw it away. Her mood did not improve when my paternal grandmother, who was staying with us, wryly remarked, "Ayalathe veetti kondu poyi thinnolum!" ("He will take it home and eat it.") Looking back, even if she suspected that it had been polluted, all that my mother had to do was to take off the top two layers!

Our industrious gardener oversaw our rabbit house as well. We had a little brick and wire mesh structure that housed about thirty rabbits and counting. Boy, could they breed! The white little bunnies were a source of constant amusement for the kids. Mom's orders to the gardener were to bring two bunnies skinned and ready to be cooked every Sunday to the kitchen. We enjoyed the rabbit curries and stew that my mother made. Then one day, one of my father's distant relatives, an old aunt from Paroor, came to visit. She was a country woman and would take my father aside to ask for money. When lunchtime came, my mother invited her to the table. Mom was about to serve a good helping of rabbit curry when the old lady asked what it was. "Ithe moyalaa (This is rabbit)," my mother replied proudly, and our guest sprang back like she had been bitten by a snake. "Ayyo, venda venda, paandurogam varum!" ("Oh no, I don't want it, you can get vitiligo from eating it!") Vitiligo is a skin disease where you get big white patches on your skin, and in India, where leprosy was still not fully eradicated, this was something that people feared. There is no scientific evidence that eating rabbits causes one to get vitiligo. But try saying that to a few eight to thirteen year olds who collectively looked down at their plates and refused to eat rabbit from then on.

Rabbit Stew

Ingredients:

1 rabbit, cleaned and cut into pieces

Salt to taste

1 onion, chopped

6 garlic cloves, chopped

1 teaspoon of crushed black pepper

1 teaspoon of garlic powder

3 sprigs of rosemary

1 tablespoon chopped fresh chives

2 tablespoons chopped fresh parsley

1 teaspoon of oregano

1 stick of butter

1 cup pearl onions

1 cup carrots

1 cup celery

1 cup frozen green peas

1 cup hearty burgundy

½ cup heavy cream

½ cup vegetable oil for browning

3 cups water

In a saucepan at medium-high heat, pour half a cup of vegetable oil and brown the pieces of rabbit. Place the pieces on a cookie sheet lined with paper towel to soak up any excess oil. In a Dutch oven at medium heat, melt the butter, add the onions, garlic, and salt, and sauté until light brown. Then add the crushed black pepper, garlic powder, and oregano. Stir this for a minute and add the rosemary, chives, and parsley. Next add the pearl onions, carrots, celery, and green peas along with the rabbit and the 3 cups of water. Give it a good stir and cook it for 35 minutes at medium. At the end of 35 minutes, add the burgundy and the heavy cream, and lower the temperature to medium low. Cook for another 10 minutes. It is a delicious stew that can be eaten with bread or rice.

41

Heavenly Endeavors:
Fr. Jacek's Golabki

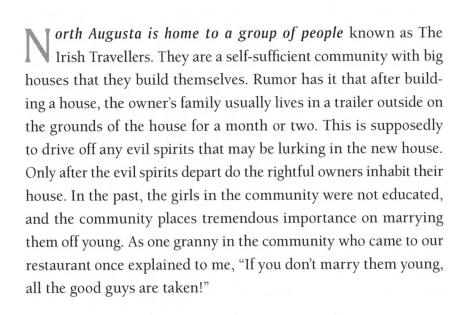

North Augusta is home to a group of people known as The Irish Travellers. They are a self-sufficient community with big houses that they build themselves. Rumor has it that after building a house, the owner's family usually lives in a trailer outside on the grounds of the house for a month or two. This is supposedly to drive off any evil spirits that may be lurking in the new house. Only after the evil spirits depart do the rightful owners inhabit their house. In the past, the girls in the community were not educated, and the community places tremendous importance on marrying them off young. As one granny in the community who came to our restaurant once explained to me, "If you don't marry them young, all the good guys are taken!"

We first met Father Cherian when he came to the café for take-out. A small man, what strikes you the most about him is his warm smile. He is the local pastor to the Traveller community, and he has been striving hard to bring about certain fundamental changes, especially where female education is concerned. Fr. Cherian has a small house in their parish of St. Edwards and has been catering to the spiritual needs of the Travellers for more than a decade now. He is also a Malayali from my home state of Kerala and is a renowned educator. After having served as the principal of two men's colleges in Kerala with a career spanning some forty years, he has retired from teaching history, which he loves. Now in his 70s, as the Vicar of St. Edwards Parish, he is continuing with aplomb on his second career. His community loves him, and they cook all the delicious dishes of the South to pamper him. The parish ladies do his laundry for him and they carefully iron even the dhotis that he wears around the house! Even with all this care, he does sometimes miss the food of his native land, Kerala, and these are the times when we have the privilege of serving him at India Café. He likes the usual Malayali fare like rice, chicken curry, and chicken biryani, but the break with tradition often comes in the form of a request for a couple of naans (the Punjabi bread) to be added to the take-out. My husband and I have been friends with him for the past seventeen years, and we have enjoyed the breadth of his vision and the vast fund of information he has accumulated from his various trips from all over the world.

When our regular Parish stopped the 12:30 Sunday mass, we started going to The Most Holy Trinity Church downtown, which had a 12:30 mass. Being restaurant owners, our Saturday nights are usually very late, and we barely slide into base even for a 12:30 mass! Holy Trinity is a beautiful old church and one of the oldest churches in the state of Georgia. Its stained glass windows are set high because it was built in days when Catholicism was not a popular religion in America and needed to withstand the stones being thrown at them! It was here that we first met Father Jacek. His sermons were always more authoritative than the usual American priest because he came from Poland as a young man, where he was brought up in the conservative traditions of the Catholic Church. He was a keen student of architecture and took pains to renovate the old church with its ancient organ, which is in the Historical Society's records, to its original grandeur. Father Jacek's first initiative was to restore all the stained-glass windows. He was then proceeding to build a big parking lot with many levels.

There is a small group of us who meet once every month for a potluck dinner, and whoever hosts it gets to pick a country or theme the dinner will be based on. One month the theme was Poland, and it was hosted by a Polish couple, so I took it upon myself to make some Golabki. I didn't even know how it was pronounced, let alone how I would go about making it. So I thought the best person to ask was Father Jacek himself. After the 12:30 mass, he would be present at the bottom of the steps to greet parishioners with a word of encouragement, a blessing or a discussion of sports. A handsome man, he was the picture of health and vitality; he was a tremendous leader too. Many a time after our trips to India and other countries, we would exchange notes on travel because he himself visited his mother twice a year in his native Poland. That Sunday when I asked him about the Golabki, he was so excited. "You put the cabbage in the pot with water and do like zis . . ." As usual his words ran into each other when he was enthusiastic, and the Germanic Z becomes more pronounced! I thanked him and made it for the potluck supper, and I must say it came out very well. Soon afterwards, Father Jacek was diagnosed with stage IV colon cancer, and he started undergoing chemotherapy. I could see him literally becoming a shadow of his former self. He stopped coming out to the steps after mass because chemotherapy left him compromised in his immunity. I had gone to India to take care of my father that summer, and when I came back I learned that father Jacek had passed away. He was only forty-seven years old. He was taken to his beloved mother and the native land he loved so much. I can never make this dish without remembering the enthusiasm with which he described it to me.

Golabki

Ingredients:

1 big white cabbage (the bigger the better because it will have bigger leaves and will be easy to roll)

1 pound of ground lamb

1 cup of half-cooked rice

1 onion, chopped

6 garlic cloves, chopped

4 tablespoons parsley, chopped

4 tablespoons basil, chopped

2 teaspoons dry oregano

1 jar of spaghetti sauce

2 teaspoons ground black pepper

2 teaspoons garlic powder

1 teaspoon crushed red pepper

¼ cup olive oil

Salt to taste

1 tablespoon of sugar

In a bowl, mix the lamb, rice, salt, half the onion, half the garlic, 2 tablespoons of parsley, 2 tablespoons of basil, 1 teaspoon of oregano, 1 teaspoon of garlic powder, 1 teaspoon of ground black pepper, and keep it aside. Fill ¾ of a pot with water and heat it at medium-high till it comes to a boil. Meanwhile, take out the core of the cabbage with a knife by making a round incision at the base of the cabbage. Then place it in the boiling water for about 5 minutes at which time take it out and put it in a colander. In about 5 minutes, the cabbage will have cooled down, and the leaves can be separated. Lay each leaf down on a flat surface, and with a sharp knife make sure that the protruding veins are shaved thin so that the leaf is easy to roll. Take a spoonful of the lamb mixture and place it at one end of the leaf. Then start rolling it, and after one rotation, fold in the two ends toward the middle just like you do for an eggroll. Finish rolling it and place it with the open side down in a rectangular casserole dish sprayed with Pam.

To make the sauce, in a saucepan at medium heat, pour in the olive oil and add the rest of the onions, garlic, 2 tablespoons of basil, 2 tablespoons of parsley, 1 teaspoon of oregano, 1 teaspoon of ground black pepper, 1 teaspoon of garlic powder, 1 teaspoon of crushed red pepper, and sauté for a few minutes. Then add your spaghetti sauce and 1 tablespoon of sugar. Pour this mixture over the dish of cabbage rolls. Cover it with aluminum foil and put it in the oven at 350° for about 45 minutes until it starts to bubble. It is a meal by itself!

Naan

Ingredients:

3 cups all-purpose flour

2 teaspoons yeast

1 tablespoon of sugar

2 tablespoons baking powder

1 teaspoon of salt

¼ cup of vegetable oil

¼ cup of plain yogurt

¾ cup of water

Put ¼ cup of water in the microwave for 40 seconds. Take it out and dissolve the 2 teaspoons of yeast in the warm water. Take out your Kitchen Aid mixer with the dough hook attachment, and into its bowl put the all-purpose flour, baking powder, sugar, salt, yogurt, and vegetable oil, and start kneading it at low speed. Then add the yeast that has been dissolved and increase the speed slowly, adding in little increments the rest of the water. Increase the speed to maximum and make sure the dough is kneaded well; you can tell this when it starts to form a smooth ball of dough. Add more water if necessary. Take out the ball of dough and place it in a bowl sprayed with Pam. Cover it with aluminum foil and let it rest in a warm place for about 6 hours at which time it will increase in volume.

Heat an iron griddle over the stove at medium temperature. Make balls of dough (the size of golf balls) and spread it in the shape of a tortilla using a rolling pin. Make it as thin as possible. With a brush, coat the surface of the heated pan with a touch of water and place the rolled-out naan on it. Cover it with a dome cover that is slightly less than the circumference of the pan. This will produce a Tandoor effect. After 40 seconds, open the lid and bubbles will have started appearing on the surface of your naan. Flip it over and put the lid back on for another 40 seconds at which time when you open the lid the bubbles would have charred slightly.

You can brush the warm naan with a mixture of softened butter, garlic powder, dried parsley, dried chives, and dried Italian seasoning. Serve warm.

42

The Hunter and the Bicycle: Lamb Stew and Appam

John Kolaf was a plantation owner near Chaalakudy, which was about ten miles from our company compound in Koratty. His parents were Australian, and he was either born in India or came to India as a very little boy. His skin was nut brown from years of weathering in the Indian sun; he was tall with crinkly eyes and an Aussie gait. He spoke Malayalam like a native and all the workers called him "Kolaappu Saippu" (Kolaf Sahib) in deference to his Caucasian ancestry. He was also a member of the Madura Coats Club and was many a time a constant fixture at the bar. He was about my father's age and whenever he would come out of the bar and see me going toward the tennis courts, he would jauntily say, "Endaadee Priye, endu parayunu?" ("Hey, Priya, how are you?") In the Malayalam language only the laboring class used phrases such as, "Dee, Podi" to address someone. The crudeness of his language would always throw me off, but I guess he learned Malayalam at an early age from the workers in his plantation!

John Kolaf and Dad were drinking buddies, and sometimes they went out hunting as well. My dad, and especially my brother, were very good with an air rifle, and they took down many a squirrel that would come to gnaw away at our ripe mangoes. In fact, my brother became so good at it, and my mother got so fed up with cleaning sometimes two squirrels in an hour, that she taught him how to skin the squirrel, marinate it, and fry it himself.

Dad and John Kolaf, however, were in search of bigger game. They were hunting for the Indian bison in the small forests near Vaalayaar. My mother never approved of my father's association with the fun-loving Aussie. I remember when dad returned from a hunt and all of us children ran down the twenty or so steps from the house to the road below. With great aplomb, Dad opened the bubble-like trunk of his Land Master car and called out to mom to send the cook to take up all the bison meat. This meat would later be packaged in the big leaves of a root vegetable plant, bundled together with coir strings, and tied up on the roof over the wood burning stove for it to dry and turn into a kind of jerky. But the big surprises were still in the car trunk. When we peered into the car there was a little lamb standing up just as it would in a field of grass! They had also shot the little lamb and by the time it arrived home, rigor mortis had set in.

I can only imagine the horror of a scene like this in the present day! But we were children growing up in India, and our food was both locally sourced and locally butchered. So this did not particularly bother us. We even played a little with the lamb. Then Daddy took out his next surprise. It was a red two-wheeler bicycle with training wheels, all wrapped up in a newspaper. You can imagine the excitement of all the kids as they took turns riding it. Dad had a particular technique for training us in this aspect as well. The road was a little inclined where we lived, so he would take us to the top of the incline, hold onto the seat, and tell us to go down. Confident of his grip, we would pedal down only to realize when we got there, that he had let go halfway down!

Appam and lamb stew is a classic combination that is served as a first course in all Kerala feasts. Sometimes when the number of diners got too big, they would resort to bread and lamb stew, but the real tradition is the Kerala bread known as "appam" with its characteristic soft fluffy middle and the thin lace-like ends more like a crepe'. The small appam pan in which this is made is available in all Indian stores.

Lamb Stew

Ingredients:

2 pounds of lamb stew meat, washed with salt and water to take away any gamey smells

3 big potatoes peeled, washed, and cut into chunks

Salt to taste

1 onion, thinly sliced

1 teaspoon turmeric powder

1 teaspoon chili powder

1 teaspoon garlic powder

1 teaspoon ground black pepper

1 teaspoon onion powder

2 tablespoons apple cider vinegar

2 green chilies, vertically slit in the middle

1 finger length of ginger, chopped

Four pods cardamom

Six cloves

2 cinnamon sticks

4 star anise

3 bay leaves

1 teaspoon allspice seeds

1 onion, chopped

3 garlic cloves, chopped

2 tablespoons curry leaves

2 cans of unsweetened coconut milk

3 tablespoons coconut oil

3 cups water

In a pressure cooker, put the washed lamb, salt, turmeric powder, chili powder, garlic powder, ground black pepper, onion

powder, apple cider vinegar, and 3 cups of water, close the lid, and set the heat to medium-high. When the steam escapes at the top, put the weight on and continue cooking for 15 minutes at medium heat. The lamb will be tender. In a pot, boil the potatoes with water and salt for 15 minutes. Drain and add them to the pressure cooker with the cooked lamb. To this add the sliced onion, green chili, ginger, cardamom, cloves, cinnamon, star anise, allspice, bay leaves (leave the last six spices starting with cardamom whole and not powdered), and the coconut milk. Cook it covered for about 10 minutes at medium heat until everything blends together. In a small saucepan at medium-high heat, pour in the coconut oil and add the chopped onion, garlic, and curry leaves. Sauté until golden brown then add it to the stew to enhance the flavor. Give it a good stir.

Appam (Rice Bread)
Ingredients:

1 cup long-grain rice, soaked in water for 6 hours

2 cups rice flour

1 packet unsweetened grated coconut

Salt to taste

4 tablespoons sugar

2 teaspoons dry yeast

2 cups water

In half a cup of water heated for 40 seconds in the microwave, dissolve the yeast. Put the drained long-grain rice along with the unsweetened coconut, salt, and 2 cups of water in a blender and blend it until smooth. Empty the contents of the blender into a bowl and add the 2 cups of rice flour and sugar. With a whisk, blend everything smoothly, cover it with aluminum foil, and keep it in a warm place for 6 hours. When you open it up, you will see a fermented batter that is ready to pour. Into a small appam pan (we call it an appachatty) sprayed with Pam at medium low heat, pour four tablespoons of batter, then quickly take the pan off the stove and rotate it in a circular motion; you will find that there will be a thick mound of batter in the middle of the pan and a thin lace of batter around it. Put the pan back on the stove, close the lid, and wait for about 3 minutes until the bottom of the appam would have started to brown. Open the lid and scoop it up and into a platter. This fluffy bread can be served with any stews or curries.

43

Catfish Beer and Ishq:
Steak and Baked Potato

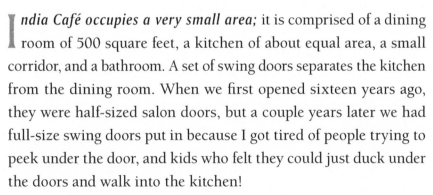

ndia Café occupies a very small area; it is comprised of a dining room of 500 square feet, a kitchen of about equal area, a small corridor, and a bathroom. A set of swing doors separates the kitchen from the dining room. When we first opened sixteen years ago, they were half-sized salon doors, but a couple years later we had full-size swing doors put in because I got tired of people trying to peek under the door, and kids who felt they could just duck under the doors and walk into the kitchen!

Over the years we have had several people working at the café, and they have all put their stamp on the business. I believe that is the reason India Café has remained a casually elegant but still a bohemian restaurant. Because of the difficulty we faced due to being a small facility, we were hiring waitresses at $8.25 an hour when minimum wage was only $5.15 an hour, and even then it was hard to find people who had enough basic social skills and enough literacy who could work at a certain level with a little bit of training. Our very first waitress was an older country lady named Betsy from a very rural area, and her only idea of Indian cooking was that it is mind-bogglingly hot! One night, a middle-aged Indian couple had come in and Betsy walked into the kitchen and announced that the gentleman has specifically said to make his lamb vindaloo very spicy. As if to emphasize the point she told me, "'Burn my ass up!" That's what he said, and not knowing any better I made the vindaloo fairly spicy. After all the tables have been served, I usually like to go into the dining area and chat with some of the guests. When we first opened the café', in my naïveté, sometimes I would go and greet a guest in between service, especially if they were also acquaintances. But then would come a barrage of unflattering comments on Yelp like, "The chef was busy talking to a table while I was waiting for my food!" So now I have made it a policy that socializing has to wait till all the tables are served. That night after dishing up the vindaloo, when I got a chance to enter the dining room, I found a very unhappy Indian guy who was dabbing his forehead with a handkerchief and trying to drink as much water as possible to soothe his tongue, which was on fire!

Tikki was our first cook. A graduate of the Akin culinary school, she was passionate about Indian cooking and she was a fast learner. She was young, energetic, and interested in the customers; I was sure that she would take over the kitchen after a few years. But she was having some family issues and had to move on. Even much later, when I would see her at the local arts festival, she would ask me if I had any openings for a cook.

Sabrina, the next in line, was a seasoned waitress, tall and strong, and able to do most of the work with ease. She had a jolly nature and I would hear her in the dining hall laughing away as she shared a joke with some guest. Sabrina really liked the old Hindi song and dance videos that I play in the café. Somehow she figured that the word "Ishq" means "love," so when the dinner service would be over at 8:30 in the evening, she would start jiving and singing at the top of her voice, "Ishq, ishq!" competing with the romantic movie hero, Sharukh Khan. It was at this time that there was a major derailment of a train carrying caustic chemicals that sent out toxic vapors in a small town in Georgia, and the company was offering very high wages to those who wanted to clean up the mess in hazmat suits. Sabrina chose to go and work there so that she could make a lot more money.

Then there was a cook whom the country waitress called "One-Eyed Tommy" because he was blind in one eye. He had been a line cook all his life and he felt that he knew it all. One of his jobs was to grill chicken tikka pieces on the big, commercial griddle. Now, anyone who is familiar with grilling knows that you have to give the meat enough time to build a char. Tommy would keep flipping it this way and that, and it always seemed like he was fighting with the chicken. I tried telling him to go slow, but he would not listen, so one day when I saw him having the usual tug-of-war on the griddle, in irritation I made the mistake of telling him, "What did the chicken do to you? Why can't you just leave it alone?" This offended him so much that he walked out of the kitchen that day and never came back!

Jeannie, the next waitress we had, was the most bizarre of all of them. She told me that she had been married to a guy from Pakistan and had a child by him. Jeannie claimed that was what got her interested in Indian cooking because Pakistan and India share much of the same food culture. When a few weeks went by, she told us how her daughter had been molested by her Pakistani husband and how he was trying to take the girl away from Jeannie to bring her up according to the Islamic traditions. I felt sorry for her and tried to commiserate and cheer her up. Even for my naïve self, though, it was too much when she started talking about the FBI boarding the plane and yanking away her crying child from its terrible father and reuniting the baby with her! Where had I seen this movie before?

Isaac was our 350-pound cook, and in my narrow kitchen when he was at work, I did not even have room to pass through. With his weight he found it hard to do most jobs, and I can still see him resting on one elbow at the edge of the three-compartment sink while washing dishes! My parents were visiting us from India at this time, and they felt like he was lazy. My mother, who was always trying to look out for me, would try to find things that needed to be done in the café in order to get him to work. So when Isaac saw my mother walking down the parking lot toward the café he would sarcastically comment, "Here comes Granny!"

The next waitress we had was a Whoopi Goldberg look-alike. She was a heavy smoker and a daily lottery player, and when I sometimes advised her not to spend so much of her tip money on gambling, she would jauntily tell me, "You can't win if you don't play!" She was illiterate and would bring me condolence cards for friends and family who had lost loved ones and wanted me to write, "First be sayin', to the most respected family members, God be with ya'll. He be going on to heaven, don't ya'll worry about it, love to ya'll, signed, Fannie Mae." She would painstakingly write out her name at the end. When a customer ordered something, she would try to eyeball where the dish was on the menu and would try to point it out to me in the kitchen. It was a tenuous system and didn't last very long. One night during service, one of the customers wanted a Kingfisher beer. She came into the kitchen and told me that the end table had wanted a "Catfish beer!" Fannie Mae lived in public housing, and her stories of gangs, violence, and drugs were eye-opening to say the least.

Most of my kitchen staff was not crazy about Indian food. At the end of service when I asked them what they wanted to eat, most of them would choose a Tandoori chicken wrap that was the closest thing to a sandwich. On weekends, I would get all of us T-bone steaks and grill them along with onions and bell peppers. I'd make baked potatoes to go along with them. This was something that all of them looked forward to. But while my husband and I always ate our steaks medium rare, Fannie Mae would take hers back to the grill and incinerate it, because she said, "It ain't cooked!"

T-bone Steaks

Ingredients:

8 ounce T-bone steaks with bone in

Salt to taste

½ teaspoon black pepper

½ teaspoon garlic powder

½ teaspoon onion powder

½ teaspoon Chinese five spice powder

1 teaspoon chopped dry chives

1 teaspoon chopped dry parsley

1 teaspoon Italian seasoning

1 teaspoon balsamic glaze

1 teaspoon soy sauce

½ teaspoon Sriracha sauce

2 teaspoons vegetable oil

1 onion, sliced

1 green bell pepper, sliced

Rub all the ingredients (except the onions and bell peppers) onto your steak and let sit for 10 minutes. On a heavy iron griddle pan heated to medium low, place the steaks and cook on each side for five minutes each. Then place the griddle in the center rack of an oven heated to 350° for 10 minutes. Your steaks will be medium rare. Sauté the onions and bell peppers in oil and the steak will look good when served on a bed of caramelized onions and bell peppers.

Baked Potatoes
Ingredients:

4 large russet baking potatoes, washed and dried

½ stick of butter

¼ cup sour cream

¼ cup cheddar cheese

Salt

1 teaspoon black pepper

1 teaspoon garlic powder

2 teaspoons chopped chives

2 teaspoons chopped parsley

Place the potato in the center of a microwave, cover it, and let it cook for six minutes. Then turn it over and bake it for six more minutes. If you run a fork into the middle of it, you can tell if it's cooked all the way through. When the potato is soft to the touch, slit the middle and compress the ends to make the middle gap bigger. Put the butter, salt, pepper, and garlic powder in first and then the sour cream and cheese. Top it with a sprinkling of chives and parsley.

44

A Welcome to the New In-laws: Lisa's Wine

George, my husband's nephew, is getting married. It is an arranged marriage, and the bride, a young lady from a very good family with affluent connections, is also a professional information technologist like him. They have met just once in her home amongst parents, siblings, and numerous other relatives. The two young people seemed to like each other, and the next step is a formal engagement in church witnessed by a priest. In the past, there would be no connection between the betrothed either by phone or in person, such as going out to a restaurant to eat. Nowadays most of them chat on the phone or text each other, although very few of them still will be seen in public together before the actual wedding. This is also a safeguard for the reputation of the young people involved in case the wedding falls through (and this was also a possibility because of malicious gossip or the sudden revelation of mental illness, previous romantic dalliances, or family skeletons in the closet), so that no lasting harm would be done. But George and Susan were meant to be together, and at last the wedding day has arrived!

The groom and the bride have been in makeup—yes, even the groom undergoes makeup rituals such as fine barbering, evening out skin tones, defining eyebrows and the like. This is a new phenomenon which did not exist in our days—since 5 o'clock in the morning in their respective towns. After a hurried breakfast of appam and mutton stew, it is time for the formal tearful goodbyes, and then it's off to church in the car decorated with flowers. There are some five hundred guests milling around in church waiting for the grand entrance of the bride and groom. Photographers are clicking away from the back of a pickup truck, and there are two drone experts flying their overhead drones to get an aerial view of the whole ceremony. It is a high mass with lots of singing (the choir doing a fantastic job and the priest not such a fantastic one), and there are instances of where the Hindu culture has seeped in to the Catholic wedding. For instance, the groom ties a "thaali" or gold chain with a cross embossed on a little heart-shaped pendant around the bride's neck and presents her with a beautiful gold-worked sari as a symbolic gesture of his responsibility as a husband, to take care of her for the rest of her life. Unlike in the Western weddings, there is not a whole lot of smiling and the whole situation is rather tense until they finish signing in the church registry. Then you can see the atmosphere visibly relaxing, and everybody gets into a party mood. Weddings are lavish affairs in India, and for this wedding the whole stage was decorated with live orchids hanging from the ceiling. It was beautiful. The lunch was equally sumptuous with at least twenty Indian vegetarian and non-vegetarian dishes and three or four kinds of breads, an Italian buffet, and a Chinese buffet, not to mention the elaborate dessert table. There were 1,500 guests at the event!

My brother-in-law Vincent is a very popular internist in Chaavakkad. Energetic and totally dedicated, he has patients who come to see him from all the neighboring towns. He is a typical Indian practitioner whose clinic is adjoined to his house. When you go to visit him and his wife in their beautiful home, you can see the long line of outpatients who queue up early in the morning to be able to consult with him. His wife Lisa grew up on a big farm where they had every kind of livestock known to man and grew several acres of farm products. She carries on this same industriousness as the doctor's wife as well, and her home always has so many interesting things to see. The big fish tank in the foyer is always kept spotless with huge, lazy fish swimming around, and you can hear the sound of some twenty parakeets bustling about in their area fenced off with wire mesh. Numerous exotic plants and fruit trees grow in her yard. She is also an excellent cook.

After the wedding reception, the groom's immediate family hurries to their house because it is time to welcome the new bride and her family to the groom's home for the first time. This is also the first time the bride will get to see her husband's home. Lisa is bringing out her best after-dinner liquor glasses in order to serve her famous homemade wine. The guests will be served cake and wine when they enter the house. But before that, as the new bride gets out of the car in the porch and takes her first tentative step (always putting forth the right leg because it is considered auspicious) into the house, the mother-in-law (Lisa) presents her with a small diamond necklace and garlands both the groom and the bride with strands made of rose petals. There are formal words exchanged where the mother of the bride joins the hands of the bride and her new mother-in-law, and entrusts her to look after the young girl.

Lisa's wine made with grapes was splendid, so I had to find out the recipe. I propose to make my wine with cherries and peaches because the colors are spectacular, and it is a good balance between the sweet and the tart.

Homemade Wine

Ingredients:

6 pounds of cherries, washed

12 ripe peaches, washed and pitted

3 packets of Brewer's yeast

4 cups sugar

2 teaspoons salt

2 egg whites

4 cinnamon sticks

10 cloves

6 star anise

12 cups water

In half a cup of water, dissolve the yeast packets and stir it well. In a food processor, put the cherries in, pit and all, and just bruise them (do not over blend for this will produce cloudy wine). Do the same thing with the peaches. In Kerala the housewives have elaborate Chinese jars of clay for winemaking. I have never been a big fan of these porous jars for winemaking, so I use a clean steel cylindrical container with an airtight lid. It is into this that I pour the contents of the food processor along with the sugar, salt, beaten egg whites (this is to clarify the wine at the end) along with the yeast, cinnamon, cloves, star anise, and the 12 cups of water. Stir it well and keep it in a cool place like a basement with the lid closed tightly. This has to mature for 21 days. Every day at a certain appointed time (this is an old wives' tale), open the lid and give it a good stir so that the sediments that have floated to the top can be rejoined in the liquid. After a couple of days, you will start to notice the fermentation process and slowly get the smell of new wine. On the twentieth day, do not stir it so that the sediments will settle in a mass at the top. On the twenty-first day, scoop up all the sediments on the top and discard it. Pour the liquid through a cheese cloth into another sterilized bowl. While pouring, discard the yeast sedimentation at the bottom of the steel container. For a deeper color, you can caramelize sugar in a saucepan and when it turns a dark brown, turn off the heat, pour half a cup of brandy into it, and empty this syrup into the new wine in the bowl. Using a funnel, you can fill the bottles with the new wine and, closing it tightly, put them away in a dark place. In about 10 days, this wine needs to be poured into other bottles so that the sediments again can be thrown away. Sometimes this process has to be repeated one more time before the wine becomes clearer. Then keep the bottles in a cool dark place. The more aged the wine becomes, the stronger the flavor will be. Chin-Chin!

45

Over and Above: Tomato Chutney

Amudha is my father's cook and housekeeper. My father has been bedridden for the last couple of years. At 92, he has severe dementia and is not capable of any kind of movement. So he is being cared for in an apartment in Bangalore by Amudha and a rotating roster of male nurses. All of my siblings take turns staying at the apartment and overseeing his care. Every six months or so when I am visiting, at 8 o'clock in the morning, the doorbell will chime, and through the monitor I can see Amudha's round smiling face with her single braid of hair; she wears a colorful sari and a stylish blouse to match, which she would have purchased on the foot path markets at rock-bottom prices! Don't let the beguiling smile fool you because underneath it there is a razor-wit and a country wisdom born out of years of having to make do. The first thing after removing her slippers outside the door of the apartment is to come bustling in with queries of, "Enna Priyamma, Breakfastuke enna venam?"("Hi Priya Madam, what do you want for breakfast?") She will go first to my mother's picture on a side table and lay a small handful of jasmine flowers at the foot of it, flowers she would have plucked in the garden below the apartment complex when the watchman was not looking! Holding her palms together, she will invoke the blessings of my mother who passed away two years ago.

Then it is on to the kitchen to get breakfast ready. In between there will be a running commentary on all the activities in the city—a work stoppage here, her neighbor being arrested for wife abuse, the steep auto rickshaw fares, and news about any politician visiting their neighborhood. She considers herself a bit of an activist in her circle and uses political parties on either side to get things done in their "hulli" or village by promising to vote for them! By this time, Dad's nurse would have bathed him and brought him to the dining table in a wheelchair. Amudha would very grandly put a steaming plate of idlis (rice cakes) with tomato chutney in front of my father. She would put her face close to his and ask him in her best English, "Meester, Pulose, how er yuuu? Idli venama?" ("Do you want idlis?") And she will keep haranguing him till she gets a response in the form of a nod or a laugh from my father. In India where a bedridden patient is usually catered to and not much interacted with, she shows a tremendous dedication and a great deal of heart in trying to get some reaction from my dad. I am also amazed at the level of sophistication this country woman—who has probably not had more than fifth grade level education—exhibits in dealing with the situation. Time and time again when my father sometimes deteriorates to a point where we are worried if he will even make it, I have seen

Amudha interact with him, figure out what he needed, and pull him out of the abyss.

Amudha, when she was young , fell in love with a man her parents did not approve of. So she ran off with him, got married, and had three girls from him. He proved to be a good-for-nothing and Amudha was left with the task of looking after the family. Amudha's three daughters are all graduates, and she explained to me how she was able to educate them. She told me that she had heard of this program when the girls were young, so she sent a letter explaining her impoverished situation (which the social worker helped her to write) to America along with pictures of the girls. She is grateful for the kindhearted person in America who adopted her girls and sent money regularly for their food, clothes, and education. She is an eternal optimist and rules over her kingdom, which extends to the rotating nurses, the watchman below, the milkman, the paper supplier, the doctor who comes for home visits to check on my dad, and all the other ancillary services, like a benevolent despot. If the home nurse does not do her bidding, he will find himself put on a diet as she handles the food supply chain too!

Amudha was thrilled that I loved her tomato chutney. "Amerikkavile hotelilel serve pannide." ("Serve it in your hotel in America.") In India, especially among the uneducated, hotel and restaurant are interchangeable because the masses in India have never stayed in a hotel, but even daily laborers will buy chai or a dosa from roadside stalls called hotels.

Tomato Chutney

Ingredients:

12 tomatoes, washed and cubed

Salt to taste

6 shallots, chopped

3 garlic cloves, chopped

3 green chilies, chopped

1 finger length of ginger, peeled and chopped

3 tablespoons cilantro, chopped

3 tablespoons curry leaves

6 tablespoons coconut oil

2 tablespoons black mustard seeds

½ teaspoon turmeric powder

½ teaspoon chili powder

6 pods of dried chili

2 tablespoons roasted Bengal Gram (pottu kadala)

In a saucepan at medium-high heat, pour in 3 tablespoons of coconut oil and add the shallots, garlic, ginger, green chilies, Bengal gram, and chopped cilantro. When the mixture gets a little color, add the salt, turmeric powder, and chili powder. Brown it for a minute and then add the cubed tomatoes. In about three minutes the tomatoes will start breaking down. At this time turn off the stove, put the mixture in a blender and blend it until smooth. In a smaller saucepan at medium-high heat, pour in the other 3 tablespoons of coconut oil, and when the oil gets hot, add the mustard, curry leaves and the dried chili pods. When the mustard

seeds start popping, pour this seasoned oil into the tomato mixture and stir. This is a great chutney to serve with idlis, dosas, or any kind of pakoras.

46

Missionaries' Contribution:

Achappam, Kozhalappam, Vatteppam, and Appam

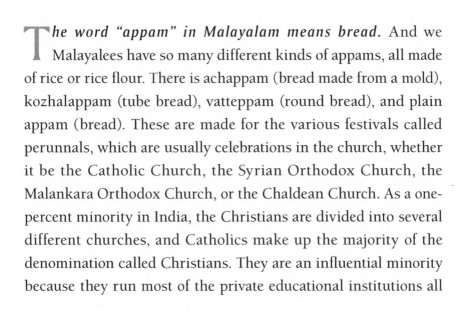

The word "appam" in Malayalam means bread. And we Malayalees have so many different kinds of appams, all made of rice or rice flour. There is achappam (bread made from a mold), kozhalappam (tube bread), vatteppam (round bread), and plain appam (bread). These are made for the various festivals called perunnals, which are usually celebrations in the church, whether it be the Catholic Church, the Syrian Orthodox Church, the Malankara Orthodox Church, or the Chaldean Church. As a one-percent minority in India, the Christians are divided into several different churches, and Catholics make up the majority of the denomination called Christians. They are an influential minority because they run most of the private educational institutions all over India. The priests travel all over the world, and they go back and forth between the Vatican and Kerala frequently. This has been going on for some time.

We have also had the influences of many European missionaries, especially from France, Italy, and Portugal coming over to work either in actual mission work tending to the sick and impoverished, or as educators working in the institutions belonging to the churches. These are the influences that have shaped many of these breads in Kerala. An achappam is a native version of the pinwheel cookies made in France; kozhalappam is very similar to the Italian cannolis (the only difference being that it is not sweet); vatteppam is the native Malayali cake; and appam is made very much like the French crepes.

For a Perunnal, the church is decorated with bright banners and all the idols are garlanded and extra candles lit. Usually it is a festival of the patron saint of that particular church, and it is an important enough occasion to warrant the arrival of His Eminence, the bishop. There will be a high mass and the church grounds will be filled with vendors of all kinds, selling tooting plastic horns, glass bangles of every variety, sweet treats of all kinds, and balloons twisted to form fantastic shapes of poodles and cats. As kids we were all familiar with the particular vendor who sold candies of such a vibrant pink color that it would leave its stain in your mouth for days after the Perunnal! It was a time when most local families invited their kith and kin from other towns to come and stay with them and celebrate. Housewives would start gearing up for the festival months in advance, making achappams and kozhalappams and storing them away in tall two-foot-high kerosene tin containers. Not having Tupperware like now, they meticulously washed out these tall containers and dried them in the sun to get rid of the kerosene smell. There were special cooks who specialized in going door to door helping to make these treats since they had to be made in very large numbers, like two hundred and three hundred each, and stored in these airtight containers to maintain the crispiness. A week before the Perunnal, the woman of the house will embark on making the more perishable breads, like vatteppam and appam.

The number of these products made was also the status symbol of a family. In Kerala, it is traditional for the woman to go to her childhood home to deliver her baby. The rationale was that her mother and relatives would provide a better environment for her to go through the laborious process of childbirth and of providing care afterward. When the woman delivers her baby, her family literally sends basket loads of these treats to her husband's family as a joyful way of announcing the birth. Sometimes taxis are hired to take five hundred achappams, five hundred kozhalappams, fifty vatteppams, and other treats for the in-laws that the mother-in-law gets to distribute among her relatives! They were painstakingly made one at a time late into the night, with big vats of oil involved, in a huge vessel called an "urili." Made in days when sugar, flour, and oil were not only in short supply but were also quite expensive, it was quite a production!

Achappam
(Bread Made in a Mold)

Ingredients:

2 cups all-purpose flour

¼ cup rice flour

Salt to taste

1 cup sugar

2 tablespoons vanilla extract

2 tablespoons sour cream

1 can of coconut milk

12 cups of vegetable oil for frying

In a bowl, put the rice flour, all-purpose flour, vanilla, sugar, salt, sour cream, and coconut milk and whisk briskly. It has to be the consistency of pancake batter. Add more water if necessary. Heat the oil in a wok to 325°. When the oil is hot enough, dip the flower mold into the oil and then quickly dip it in to the batter, making sure that the mold does not immerse all the way to the top in the batter. Then quickly dip the mold into the oil, and you will see the little florets separating from the mold in the oil. Scoop them up when they start to brown. If you immerse the mold completely in the batter, the florets will not be able to separate from the mold in oil. Place the achappams thus made on a plate lined with paper towels.

Kozhalappams
(Tube Bread)

Ingredients:

3 cups rice flour

6 shallots, minced

3 garlic cloves, minced

Salt to taste

1 teaspoon garlic powder

1 teaspoon ground black pepper

2 teaspoons black cumin seeds

2 tablespoons black mustard seeds

12 cups vegetable oil for frying

¼ cup coconut oil

¼ cup grated coconut

1 can of coconut milk

Pour the coconut oil into a saucepan set over medium-high heat. When it gets hot, put the mustard seeds in and wait until they pop. In a blender, grind the shallots, garlic, and grated coconut until smooth. To this add the garlic powder, ground black pepper, and salt and blend well. In a bowl, put the rice flour and the coconut milk and pour in the contents of the saucepan and the blender, and mix it well with your hands. Add extra warm water if necessary to make it of a smooth consistency. Break off a little ball of this dough and gently roll it out thinly with a thin rolling pin. Heat the oil in a wok to 350°. Take one of the rolled-out round pieces of dough and, using a finger or a cannoli tube, shape it into a tube-shape and drop it in the oil. Fry it for about four minutes until it is a thin, flaky, crispy tube. Place it on a plate lined with a paper towel to blot any excess oil.

Vatteppam
(Round Bread)

Ingredients:

1 cup of long-grain rice, washed and left to soak in water for 6 hours

2 cups rice flour

3 teaspoons dry yeast

½ cup sugar

Salt to taste

2 cans coconut milk

2 teaspoons Rava (cream of wheat)

1 cup water

Place a bowl with half a cup of water in the microwave for 40 seconds and dissolve the yeast into this. In another bowl with ¼ cup of water, put the 2 teaspoons of Rava and microwave it for a minute. Stir this mixture well. Blend the soaked rice in a blender until smooth along with 1 cup of water. Pour this into a bowl and add the rice flour, salt, sugar, the yeast mix, the Rava mix, and the two cans of coconut milk. Whisk it well. Cover the bowl with aluminum foil and keep it in a warm place for about 6 hours. By then the batter would have started to ferment. In a pressure cooker, pour 1 cup of water and place it on the stove at medium-high heat. Place a vegetable steamer inside the pressure cooker.

Take a round steel plate of 2-inch depth and spray it thoroughly with Pam. Stir the batter in the bowl. With a deep serving spoon, ladle spoonfuls of the batter into the plate until it is half way full. This gives the batter room to rise. Place the plate on the vegetable steamer, close the lid of the pressure cooker, and steam for 20 minutes. Do not put the weight on the lid of the pressure cooker. Carefully take out the plate with the vatteppam and give it a few minutes to cool. It will then slide off easily onto a plate with the help of a butter knife to loosen the edges. You can then cut it in the traditional wedge-shaped slices like a cake.

Appam (Bread)

This crepe-like bread has been explained
in chapter 43.

47

The Show Must Go On: Payasam (Vermicelli Pudding)

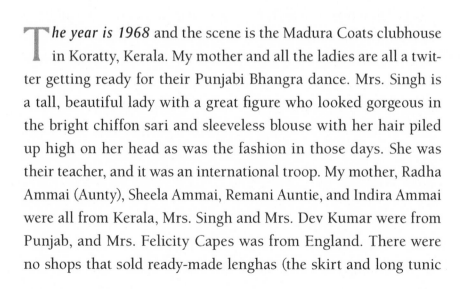

The year is 1968 and the scene is the Madura Coats clubhouse in Koratty, Kerala. My mother and all the ladies are all a-twitter getting ready for their Punjabi Bhangra dance. Mrs. Singh is a tall, beautiful lady with a great figure who looked gorgeous in the bright chiffon sari and sleeveless blouse with her hair piled up high on her head as was the fashion in those days. She was their teacher, and it was an international troop. My mother, Radha Ammai (Aunty), Sheela Ammai, Remani Auntie, and Indira Ammai were all from Kerala, Mrs. Singh and Mrs. Dev Kumar were from Punjab, and Mrs. Felicity Capes was from England. There were no shops that sold ready-made lenghas (the skirt and long tunic outfit of the North Indian ladies) in Kerala in those days, and so many chiffon saris were cut and tailored to outfit the ladies. They wore their hair in a bun on top of the head and the thin, beautifully worked veil was pinned to the top of this. It was a beautiful dance with the ladies going around in circles to the rhythm of the "dol" (ceremonial drum) with the handsome Mr. Singh, with his distinguished turban, playing the drums with flourish. My dad was in makeup for Kathakali, a local opera with exaggerated gestures. An artist had come for the purpose and was lining my father's face in the green and white paint characteristically used for this purpose. The eyes are dramatically enhanced by drawing thick lines of Kohl.

The year is 1990 and we are in the green room of the Westside school auditorium in Augusta, Georgia. It is a state of confusion and chaos. It is Onam, the biggest celebration in the Kerala calendar, where people all over Kerala remember the great king who once upon a time ruled Kerala with wisdom and justice but was put down by the gods because even they were so jealous of him. But the great Mahabali's parting wish was that he should be allowed to come back once a year to see his beloved people. So we celebrate this in the memory of a king who put the interests of his people ahead of his own. It is also celebrated at a time when the rice fields are brimming with their golden bounty and hence it is also a harvest festival. "Ende vaarumudi evide?" ("Where is my false hair?") "Ende chilanka aarengilum kandittundo?" ("Has any one seen my dancing ankle bells?") The teenage dancers are getting ready for their classic performance. On the other side, all of us ladies are dressed up in our traditional "settu mundu," the traditional off-white cotton saris with their elegant gold borders, and we are helping each other pin garlands of jasmine into our hair. Smitha, Indira, Shaji, Carol, Thresiamma, Jaya, Alice, Money, Asha, and myself, the whole gang, is huddled together practicing the steps in place one more time, before going on stage. "Ee steppine ellavarum onnu nannayittu irikkanam ketto (Everyone should really go down to the floor in this step)," Carol, the youngest of the group reminded us. Some of us who are a little older groaned at the thought of having to put our knees through that torture! My good friend Reena is busy drawing fake mustaches with an eyebrow pencil for King Mahabali and his grand entourage of six- to seven-year-olds. I see my extremely dignified husband carrying a live rooster along with his friend Joyachan because they were getting ready for a comical skit. At the other end of the room, Dr. Carmel Joseph (pulmonary specialist extraordinaire) is draping his checkered calico cloth dhoti to act in the play as a thief brought in by the policeman (played by Georgee) to the station. The men are supporting each other, trying to get ready for the traditional Kerala Boat Race, which they depict on stage. The real boat races in Kerala for the Nehru trophy are watched by even international visitors from all over the world. The long snake boats as they are called (they seem to have some resemblance to the Chinese boats, but Kerala has had long trade relations with China and evidence of this is seen in every aspect of the culture) glide through the back waters of Kerala effortlessly, each with a crew of some forty people rowing in perfect synchronization to the beat of the song. The crew consists usually of fishermen from the local villages, and they wear their wife-beater undershirts along with a dhoti that is hitched up and a thin towel wrapped around their heads. Our Augusta crew of ten oarsmen are feeling slightly self-conscious about showing off their sagging bust lines in their wife-beaters!

It is a very forgiving audience as they are also our friends and neighbors from the local area, and they congratulate us on our stellar performances. The children heave a sigh of relief that they can get out of their stifling costumes. The next event is something everyone looks forward to—the Onam Sadhya or feast. There are no plastic plates here to pollute the earth; instead, the vegetarian food is served on banana leaves. It is a conveyor belt system where the servers come one after another with various dishes and place a small amount of it in the designated areas on your banana leaf. Some of the dishes enjoyed are aviyal, kaalan, olan, theeyal, erissery, saambaar, and the list goes on and on (some of them have been mentioned in this book). In Kerala it is entirely eco-friendly since after eating, these leaves are put into a bin and the cows enjoy the Sadhya too! Here in America the leaves are put in the trash. For Onam, the dessert is always paayasam. There are several kinds, but the most memorable one is semia paayasam made with thin vermicelli and milk. Another Onam for the history books!

Paayasam (Vermicelli Pudding)

Ingredients:

1 packet of thin vermicelli (also called semia, available in Indian grocery stores)

2 cans condensed milk

½ liter of half-and-half

1 stick butter

1 cup sugar

6 cardamom pods

¼ cup cashews

¼ cup raisins

Salt to taste

3 cups water

In a deep saucepan at medium heat, melt the butter and add the vermicelli, stirring constantly to roast it (the vermicelli has to be broken with the hand into tiny pieces before adding it). When the vermicelli turns light brown, add the cashews, raisins, and cardamom and stir it for one more minute. Then add the condensed milk, half-and-half, sugar, salt, and 3 cups of water and stir it well. When the milk starts to boil, lower the heat and cook it for three more minutes until the vermicelli is nice and tender. This desert is delicious whether it is served warm or cold. If it gets too thick, just add more half-and-half or milk to thin it.

48
The End of an Era

We could see the shadows lengthening day by day. By the time 1978 rolled around, it was fast becoming evident that the Madura Coats mill at Koratty with its beautiful compound was going to be a chapter in the history of Kerala. The company paid its employees so much better than the average Indian firm that they were able to attract masters level people for even their foreman jobs. The top management trainees were mostly Indian Institute of Technology graduates who had also done their masters in business administration. Kerala is a beautiful state with an extremely fertile soil which can grow almost anything. Growing up it seemed like we hardly had to buy vegetables or fruits because they grew in our backyards. Bananas of all variety, jackfruit, mangoes of every kind, custard apples, papayas—you name it, it was freely available. The Communist Party has always ruled Kerala and they have instituted many changes for the better where the common man is concerned. They brought about land reforms, universal literacy (this is the envy of the world—we have almost 93 percent literacy!), fair wages, and working conditions, and a heightened awareness of the need to preserve nature and the planet. I remember that even as school kids, there was an Earth Day where we were encouraged by the school system to plant saplings in an attempt at reforestation.

While all these are commendable efforts, there is one aspect that had not been given much thought. In order for an industrialist to invest capital and take the risk, there has to be a return as well. Somehow in our efforts to uphold the workers' rights, we forgot to pay attention to the other side. Many factories were shut down because workers were on permanent strikes and work stoppages. It became like a teenage syndrome where you had all the rights and no responsibilities. Kerala has abundant tourism but very few industries. Most people go abroad either to the Western countries but mainly to the Middle East for work. While this is a temporary boost to the economy, it has its long-range problems as well. For example, right now with oil prices so low, I am sure that many Keralites will lose their jobs in the Middle East and will have to return home, sending the economy into a tailspin. This was what was happening with Madura Coats also. I remember my father having to hold my wedding in my grandmother's house in Trichur because the company was on lockdown due to a workers' strike. These prolonged work stoppages were affecting production and profitability, and the company decided to close its operations in Koratty. All the top management, including my father, was transferred out, and the site was returned to the government when the lease ran out. The mill was the only employer in the small town, and when they closed shop, the once-booming little town became a ghost town. People tell me that even the suicide rates went up phenomenally.

After many years of lying vacant and vandalized, an information technology park took it over, and they are using it as their offices. The company kids grew up and scattered all over the world, but some inner magnet always seems to draw us back to the place we called home. The wide streets paved with beautiful plants are sometimes overrun and the houses seem a little frayed at the edges, but almost compulsively when we go for vacations back home, most of us feel the need to go and see what once used to be a beautiful place. We get permission from the IT management to go inside the compound, and like lost souls go and knock on the door of our former homes. When a surprised and mildly curious employee opens the door, they find a middle-aged man or woman standing there wistfully saying, "I used to live here!"

49

Acknowledgments

This book would not have been possible but for the love and support given to me by my husband of forty-two years, Dr. Simon Sebastian. Although ours was an arranged marriage, his expectations of me were never limited to the traditional wife. It is true that he always liked good food, but he also always wanted me to fulfill my dreams. He patiently watched the kids when I was doing my MBA and he would even cheer me up when I got back by telling me how much my then one-week-old son missed me when I went to night classes. All through the years when we were raising a young family, he was the dad, our pillar of strength, who never lost his temper or was impatient, even when a young son in his haste to start the barbecue faster set the whole thing ablaze, or his daughter the teenager decided that she was going to be a grunge queen! Maybe it is because he is a psychiatrist trained with a psychoanalytical orientation and has for over forty long years seen enough vagaries in human nature! To me he is always my husband, ever supportive, and always helpful. During the 90s and early 20s when we were both highly involved in the Kerala Association, even though he had no interest in stage or theater, he was still happy to oblige and participate when we needed the numbers!

Sebastian has always been convinced that I had a story to tell, and he always encouraged me to start writing. When the pandemic struck and the restaurant had to be closed for a while, he was the one who got me the Dragon and set me up on the computer. He is the guardian of the files and my proofreader, and he is also the one who has taken the initiative to have the book published. Thank you from the bottom of my heart for all that you have done for me, and I know will still do for me!

I also thank my children Kavya and Arjun along with their respective spouses Nick and Stephanie for their unwavering optimism and encouragement for this project. It is they and their children I had in mind when I wrote this book so that they will get a glimpse into my childhood and early adulthood and the kind of influences that made me who I am. I hope this book will help my little two-year-old granddaughter Arya to understand the lady she calls "Ammamma" a little better.

I had a great resource in Michele De Filippo and Ronda Rawlins and the entire team at 1106 Design for being so supportive in helping publish this book. They were always professional and yet friendly and approachable which reassured me greatly as a new author. The design team of Brian Smith had great ideas and they were successful in incorporating my vision into its best form. My editor Doran Hunter provided valuable insight in improving the message. Due to his interest in the literary as well as culinary side of things, he was of great help with his insightful editing. Thank you team 1106 Design! It was my lucky day when I came to know about you.

~ Mary Sebastian
5-5-2020

About the Author

Priya Mary Sebastian was born in Kerala, India. She passed out of Calicut University with a Bachelor degree in English Language and Literature. When she married Dr. C Simon Sebastian in 1978, she moved to the United States and has resided here since. The author also has an MBA from Centenary College of Louisiana which she completed in 1989.The family has resided in Augusta ,Georgia since then and raised their two children. She has been involved in fund raising for several area philanthropic causes such as Empty Bowl, Red Cross, Breast Cancer Society and of late providing lunches for Emergency Room personnel battling Covid-19.Always interested in arts and culture, she has organized many cultural events and has been the President of both the Kerala Association of Augusta as well as the Indo-American Cultural

Association of Augusta. One of her MBA projects became a reality sixteen years back when she opened a small 45 seat restaurant called India Café. She is still cooking and enjoying exploring the cuisines of the world.

Made in the USA
Las Vegas, NV
07 February 2021

17370164R00184